Then Are the Children Free

Then Are the Children Free

Sylvia Klope Eller

VANTAGE PRESS
New York

FIRST EDITION

All rights reserved, including the right of
reproduction in whole or in part in any form.

Copyright © 2007 by Sylvia Klope Eller

Published by Vantage Press, Inc.
419 Park Ave. South, New York, NY 10016

Manufactured in the United States of America
ISBN: 978-0-533-15542-2

Library of Congress Catalog Card No.: 2006904864

0 9 8 7 6 5 4 3 2 1

To my dear husband, Bill;
my beloved children, Karen, Pamela, Shawn, Shane;
grandchildren and great-grandchildren, too numerous
to count;
my niece and special friend, Wendy;
my "Guardian Angels," Bob and Linda; Miranda;
and Chrissy, my partner in
"Our Garden, the Father's and Mine."

A Girl and Her Dog

The small girl and her dog stand motionless,
watching the sun explode in glorious colors
beyond the western hills.
No matter that the energetic wind molds her floursack dress
against her bare, brown legs.

The dog hears the mooing of the cattle telling him
it's time to take them home.
The cattle push and shove, flicking their soiled tails at pesky flies.
Do they smell the newly pumped water?
The wind, ever busy, has sent the windmill spinning,
eager to fill the water tank.

Still the small girl watches as the sun leaves the stage
and lets the curtain of darkness
drop behind the everlasting hills.
Is she dreaming of following the sun to other places,
far away from green grass pastures?
She walks slowly along the path the dog and eager cattle take.

Pin cushion cacti prickle her bare feet,
grown hard from the freedom of no shoes.
Wet drops of warm milk, from bulging udders,
left behind on blades of grass,
brush against her bare legs as she starts to run,
eagerly sniffing the Fresh-Baked Bread Smell of home.

*Then Are the
Children Free*

1

She stood on the little hill by the fence that separated the pasture from the fields to the west, and looked at the twin hills and the Big Hill rising sharply above the surrounding prairie. The strong, hot wind blew Sophie's faded cotton floursack dress against her, outlining her sturdy little body and the bloomers which were all that she wore underneath. As she stood there gazing at the hills and the brilliant colors that streaked the evening sky, Sophie absent-mindedly picked up a pebble with her bare toes, then reached down to take it in her hand, examined it, and tossed it. It was not pretty enough to keep and put in the children's 'rock store' in the calf pasture, their favorite place to play, where only special rocks were allowed. Sophie loved the feel of the wind on her body. She loved to feel her short hair, bleached almost white from the blazing North Dakota sun, blowing back off her hot face. As she stood there she wondered, "What is behind those hills?"

Papa would soon be coming home from plowing a fireguard and she'd better get the cows home for milking. As hot and dry as it had been, fire was a great worry. In a short time a raging fire could sweep over the prairie, leaving black devastation in its wake. She started down the hill and passed the pond where the cattle usually stopped to drink as she drove them home. Now it was almost dried up. Perhaps they would move faster tonight, eager to reach the corral and the tank full of fresh, cold water. It was good the wind was strong. She could hear the windmill whirring. There would be plenty of water for the thirsty cows tonight. Goph (short for Gopher Dog) left her side and ran ahead nose down, sniffing, trying to catch a cow scent. The pasture had so many little hidden valleys where the cattle liked to hide when it was hot. He disappeared, then she heard short barks calling her, and the protesting moans of the cattle as they got to their feet and appeared out of their hiding place, with Goph at their heels. Old 'Sunday Biscuits' swayed from side to side, leaving a trail of milk from her bulging bag. Sophie ran ahead and opened the corral gate as the now-running cattle rushed to the tank, pushing and shoving each other to get there first. With her job done, she called Goph and raced him to the house just as Papa, driving his two plow horses, appeared over the little hill by the barn.

The smell of fried chicken filled the air. As Sophie opened the screen door, Mama turned from the kitchen range and smiled at her.

"Were they hiding in their usual place?"

Mama looked tired, but so pretty, with her hair escaping in tendrils from the bun on the back of her head and sweat streaking her flushed face. Sophie loved the kitchen with its smells, the old black kitchen range, the crocheted rugs, the sink under the window and the loaves of warm bread on a clean floursack towel on the zinc countertop.

"Yes, Mama, but Goph smelled them out. May I have a slice of bread, please, please? And Sunday Biscuit is leaking and needs to be milked. Shall I take the milk pails to the barn?"

The bread dripped butter and chokecherry jam as she took big, satisfying bites, using her other hand to pull the little wooden wagon with the milk pails and can clinking against each other, to the barn.

Sarai came in from the potato field, dragging a protesting Robby behind her. Her hands were grimy and her face smeared with dirt and tears. Sophie was glad she hadn't had to pull weeds today. It was her turn tomorrow. Perhaps it would rain. Sarai dropped down in the yard, giving Robby a toss that landed him on his back in the tall grass.

"Why do I always have to take him along? He wants to eat dirt and squishes bugs and rubs them on me. I hate him!"

"Anyway, Bert is bringing home a big watermelon for dinner," said Sophie consolingly.

Bert rode into the yard on Old Bess, with a grin a mile wide on his face and a huge watermelon in his arms, as he tried to keep one hand on the reins. Just then Robby let out a whoop and rose up out of the grass.

"Watermelon, watermelon! I want watermelon!"

Old Bess, startled, veered to one side and the watermelon went flying out of Bert's arms and lay in big, juicy pieces on the ground.

"Why aren't you kids at the milking? I ought to take a whip to the bunch of you. The best watermelon in the field!"

Papa came stomping toward them swinging his arms. As he passed them headed for the barn they all stood with their heads down, staring at the luscious pieces of watermelon lying on the ground. They were each ready to burst into tears. It wasn't just the loss of a feast on watermelon that was at stake, they knew, as Sarai whispered, "You know what you've done now, Bert? We'll never get to go to town Saturday night, even if the cream can is full!"

A sad little group plodded on to the corral, pulling the wagon with the milk pails after them.

* * *

Mama said nothing about the watermelon, of which the chickens and turkeys were now making a grand feast.

"Sophie, run down in the cellar and get a jar of peaches and a cup of cream." Supper was a solemn affair, with peaches and whipped cream for dessert.

The wind was dying down and the heat of the day diminished a bit. Papa tucked his pipe and the bright yellow bag of Peerless in his overall pocket, got up and headed for the hill up by the barn. The water in the old barrel was pleasantly warm from the sun, and felt good on his tired body when he got out of his clothes and climbed in the barrel. His pipe was in his mouth, his old straw hat on the back of his head; all was right with the world.

The children played hide-and-go-seek while glancing up at Papa in the barrel, knowing they'd better be in the house before he decided to climb out. Sophie always wanted to laugh when she saw him up there, silhouetted against the sunset sky. Yet it gave her a warm feeling inside to know that he was there, as if no one could come past him on the road that ran down the hill to the house. She didn't know why she felt that way, really. No one ever came but the Watkins man selling vanilla and taking back eyeglasses to be repaired, close neighbors, and sometimes Uncle Melvin and Aunt Lottie. Somehow, Papa just made her feel safe.

2

"Are you awake?" whispered Sarai.

"Yes. Why are you awake?" Sophie whispered back. "Did you hear something?" The moon threw a long path across their bed, lighting up their faces as they stared at each other, big-eyed. They climbed out of bed and tiptoed to the long, narrow east window. The world out there looked mysterious, with the full moon throwing the shadows of the trees in grotesque patterns across the calf pasture, making the rock-pile look like an unfriendly dwelling . . . perhaps an ogre's house? It was so bright that they could see the Johnsons' barn and silo beyond the calf pasture. They forgot for a moment what had awakened them. Sophie looked at Sarai and asked, "Why do they have a hip-roofed barn and a silo, and we have a barn built into the side of a hill? Are they rich and we poor?"

Sarai looked puzzled and was about to answer when the sound came again, "Whrrrrr!" They saw a huge flying creature swoop down, then rise up with a small animal dangling from its beak. Sarai laughed.

"No ghost, just a barn owl. But Sophie, do you think we'll get to go to town Saturday night?"

"I wish Bertie hadn't dropped that watermelon. Mama had to have whipped cream on peaches for dessert to keep Papa happy, so it's that much less cream in the cream can. Mama will try hard to have it filled by Saturday, but we must do our part. How about getting Bert and Robby to agree not to have cream on their grits in the morning?"

"Yes, let's! I don't like cream anyway, except in ice cream."

"Ice cream! We have to go to town! Guess what I'm going to dream of? A big two-scoop ice cream cone!"

Gazing out at the beauty of the night from the downstairs bedroom, Mama heard the whispering and the pitter-patter of bare feet on the linoleum floor. She knew what the girls were yearning for. She'd taken a chance and added some water to that darn old cream can again to fill it up, in spite of Papa's temper the last time she did it. Besides, she wanted that Saturday night trip herself.

* * *

It was Friday evening and Mama was making stew for supper.

"Bert, will you go down and get a jar of beef from the cellar?"

Sophie jumped up from where she was sitting on the bottom steps of the stairway and said, "I'll go along and bring up the potatoes and carrots."

The old outside cellar door was hard to lift up. It was beginning to sag a bit from Papa sitting there in the evening with his pipe. The damp fetid odor that arose from the cellar when the door was raised always made Sophie wonder whether that's what a person would smell like if he were buried alive. She had read a story about a man being buried alive and her heart always began to pound whenever she opened that door. Hurriedly she took potatoes out of the bin to be sprouted. She loved taking the carrots out of the sandbox; the sand was cool and clean and made her hands feel as if they had just been washed. Now for the cream can. Sophie and Bert went over to the corner where it stood and both tugged on the top, opening the can and peering in hopefully. It wasn't anywhere near being full! They looked at each other in despair.

Before Sophie went in the house she sat down on the cellar door and sprouted the potatoes, pulling out each tiny green shoot as she watched the chickens gather around and almost snatch the sprouts from her hand. Just then a familiar sound made her head snap up. One old hen had not come to be fed, but was triumphantly announcing that she had laid an egg! The egg crate—was it full? Up she jumped and ran, following the cackling sound to a clump of weeds. Parting the weeds, she saw a nest of brown eggs. Mama had told her that when hens get 'broody' they will hide a nest in a secret place and several weeks later emerge with several fluffy babies in tow. Sophie took only the warmest egg, then waded back through the weeds, startling other wayward hens. When she came into the house with a big grin on her face, her apron was filled with carrots, potatoes, and a brown egg!

The next morning, breakfast was dismal even though Papa was in a good mood. Mama put a big bowl of grits in front of each child and came around with the cream pitcher.

"No thanks, Mama. I don't feel too good."

"No thanks, Mama. Lucy Johnson says I'm too fat."

"No thanks, Mama. I get pimples when I eat too much cream."

"No 'tanks, don't want.

Mama handed each child a big slice of homemade bread, toasted and with bacon fat on it. "No butter?"

Sophie almost said, and then remembered just in time—the cream can!

Mama had a little secret smile on her face.

"Well, kids," Papa said as he got up from his chair, "you'd better get your chores and baths over with so we can start for town this evening right after supper. We need to take the cream can and egg crate in. Can't let them go another week in this warm weather."

Four mouths fell open.

"Yes, Papa," came a chorus of voices.

The table was cleared in a hurry and the children all ran to get their jobs done and lay out their good clothes. They all took turns showering in the WPA outhouse, where Mama had instructed Papa to put a tub with a hole in the bottom on the roof, attach a sprinkler to the ceiling of the outhouse, and fill the tub with water. The hot sun kept the water wonderfully warm and sure beat the old tin tub set by the stove in wintertime. They were the only family in the neighborhood with 'plumbing'!

Sophie slipped into the kitchen.

"Mama, how did the cream can get full?"

"Well," Mama said, "how did you like bacon fat on your toast?"

"It was all right, but what does that have to do with—oh, I know! No butter! You poured the cream meant for the butter churn into the cream can!"

Mama smiled her sweet smile and patted Sophie on the head.

"My smart girl! A full cream can and a full egg crate!"

* * *

The old Model T Ford went bumping over the country roads, the cream can latched on the running board and the egg crate under Robby's short legs. The sun was just going down. Oh, the excitement ahead! Saturday night was the social event of the week, when the farmers and their families came to town, bringing their produce to sell. Their cream cans were left at the train depot to be taken to the creamery in Bismarck by the next train, and their crates of eggs and home-churned butter were traded for groceries. No one in the family mentioned the absence of butter on this trip! Sophie thought of the fresh sweet butter Mama usually churned, put into a pretty mold, and right before time to leave for town, turned out on a clean cheese-cloth to be dropped into a small crock of cold water. If the cloth-wrapped butter began to soften before arrival in town, Mama would pour the water out and take the butter back home, or Mr. Leidke the grocer would put it into his cooler and he and Mama would argue over the price. Mama was proud of her pretty mold of butter, "fresher and sweeter than anyone else's!" as Papa always said.

Papa stopped at the railway station to leave the full can of cream and pick up the empty can back from the creamery; deposited Mama at Leidke's grocery store; and let the children out with a sigh of relief. Now he could join the other men on the benches outside the store. He sat down with his pipe, his Peerless tobacco, and the one bottle of beer he allowed himself on his Saturday trip to town. Politics were discussed: "What about the non-partisan league?" Crops were compared. Then their voices were lowered and Papa's hearty laugh rang out above the rest. The children knew they had better not ask for their regular five cents for ice cream cones until Papa and the other men were talking in their usual loud voices again.

Bert found his friend Eric Johnson and they sidled up

to Papa and Mr. Johnson. As long as Papa and Mr. Johnson were together, they would have no trouble getting ice cream money . . . perhaps even ten cents each!

"Here, Eric, go get yourself a cone."

"Here you go, Bert, and give your sisters and brother the other fifteen cents."

Sophie, Sarai and Robby were waiting for Bert—now for that ice cream cone! The girls ran as fast as they could so that Bert would have to take Robby with him. Having made their escape they slowed to a more dignified pace. Sauntering down the one street in town, they met the two Johnson girls, Amy and Charity, and strolled on together, each licking on a cone. They stopped in front of the old hotel upon hearing music pouring out of the dance hall.

There was a beer joint in the basement of the hotel, and the four girls squatted and peered down the stairs, trying to see what went on down there. The smoke was so thick that they couldn't see much except bodies moving through the haze. Loud voices came through the open door, a bit of singing, some words that Mama said no one should use, then someone came staggering up the steps and they fled. Sophie said wistfully, "I wouldn't want to go down there, but I wish I'd hurry up and get old enough to go up where they dance. I could dance right now. . . . " She whirled and whirled until Sarai grabbed her arm.

"Papa and Mama will never bring us again if you start acting up."

Amy Johnson said, "Let's go peek behind the hotel. You wouldn't believe what I saw there once." It was scary leaving the lit-up sidewalk, sneaking down an alley at the side of the hotel. When they got to the corner, they peeked around. They heard soft voices, saw the glow of a cigarette as it spiraled to the ground, and two bodies leaned toward each other until they looked like one big person.

"Let's go," Sophie whispered, and they all hurried back to the sidewalk, glad to be where they could see what was going on; could see their dads smoking pipes on the bench by the store.

Sophie hardly remembered the trip home. After getting into bed and pulling the cool sheet up around her neck, she thought about the secretive poeple behind the hotel, why they were back there and when she would be big enough to go to the dance hall. "Will I want to smoke when I grow up?" she asked herself. "I know I wouldn't want to be behind some dark building doing something mysterious. Papa would probably give me a whipping. No, when I grow up, I just want to dance." Sophie felt herself whirling and twirling to beautiful dance music, right into dreamland.

3

Papa was arguing with Mama about getting a goat.

"They're good to have around, keeping grass eaten down. I wouldn't have to get the horses hooked up to the mower just for this yard."

But Mama had heard that goats ate clothes right off the clothesline, as well as tin cans.

"Now how many tin cans do we ever buy with all your nice jars of canned food in the cellar?"

Papa won, and when the children saw the cute little goat that he'd bought from the neighbors on the south, Mama didn't have a chance.

Bunting, as they called him, butted Goph (Goph didn't mind), and seemed to think it was a game when Jinx the cat spat at him. Sophie loved to watch the three of them and decided to write a story about them some day, since besides being a dancer, she wanted to be a writer when she grew up. Bunting especially loved her and would follow her around everywhere, but sometimes he could be such a pest!

Sophie often had a hard time sneaking away from the other kids to read in some hidden spot, until one day she hit on a great idea. "I wonder where those big boxes are that we get groceries in?" Oh, yes, Bert had them in the granary loft, where he hid secret things in them. Well, she had much right to them as he. She threw the boxes down the ladder and hauled them over to the other side of the clothesline. The clothes were blowing in the hot wind. Bunting, who was at her heels as usual, started running at the slapping sheets, though he seemed afraid to try to grab one. At least he'd be occupied for a while. Book in hand, Sophie sat down in one of the big boxes, tilted the other one over her head for privacy (who'd ever think she was inside the box?) And opened to chapter five. She and Lorna Doone became one.

BANG!! The box over her head crashed down. She tried to shake it off when BANG!!—the box went flying and she tipped over. She looked up to see Bunting staring down at her with his head on one side, while gripped tightly between his teeth were Sophie's Sunday best pink sateen bloomers from off the line. A sheet dragged behind him.

That night in bed, Sarai and Sophie put their hands over their ears so they couldn't hear Papa and Mama's loud voices coming from downstairs. The next day, Sophie stood crying as Papa led Bunting away. He strained at the rope, looking back at her as if to say, "It was all in fun. I love you." Sophie cried, "I love you too," but Papa and Bunting had already disappeared down the road.

* * *

Mama was cleaning the parlor. Every once in a while she sat down at the piano to play "Nearer My God To Thee." Bert was pulling Robby around in the old wooden wagon, Sarai and Sophie were washing the dishes, and Papa had gone to town for a part for the disc. It had broken down while he was out working in the field. Suddenly the sound of the piano was overrun by the roar of a car, being driven as fast as a Model T could go up to the house. Papa couldn't be home yet, and wouldn't drive that fast anyway, and the Watkins man drove a big truck. Who could it be? Sophie rushed outside as the car came to a stop and Mr. Johnson jumped out, eyes wild, arms waving in the air.

"Get your mother quick . . . my wife, my wife!"

Mama was already coming out the door.

"Oh, Mrs. Watson, my wife is having the baby in our trees! I tried to get her to the hospital but she said it was too late and to get a mattress. She's out in the trees on a mattress in front of God and everybody! Why did she do this to me? Why didn't she wait?"

Mama just looked at him. Then she took off her apron, went into the house to get a clean white one, climbed into the car, and they were off in a stream of exhaust smoke. Sarai and Sophie were almost too excited to finish the dishes. Why did Mrs. Johnson insist on having her baby on a mattress in the trees? They weren't exactly sure how you had a baby but why would she have it outside if Mr. Johnson didn't want her to?

Sarai decided she was bored with the whole thing and went into Papa and Mama's bedroom to try on Mama's best dress, to see how long it would be till she could wear a grown-up dress. She was two years older than Sophie and beginning to look at grown-up clothes in the Sears Roebuck catalogue.

Sophie kept thinking about the baby. Mr. Johnson had driven the long way around because of fences. But on foot, if she cut through the calf pasture, then across the south end of the cow pasture, she could get into the back of the Johnson's grove of trees. If she crouched down there, she could watch Mrs. Johnson 'have a baby.'

As she got closer, she could hear Mrs. Johnson crying and screaming. Didn't she want the baby? Sophie saw her mother bending over, Mr. Johnson walking back and forth; and the children peeking around the corner of the house. All at once she heard her mother say loudly, "You have a beautiful boy," as she held up a red, naked, squirming body emitting loud screams.

Sophie's heart pounded. *Is that the way you have a baby?* she thought. *Just lie on a mattress and there it was? My Mama worked some kind of magic. If I ever have a baby, I want to have it on a mattress in the trees with the sun shining down.*

She ran back home and never told anyone about her experience. It became her precious secret.

* * *

It was just dusk. Papa was sitting on the cellar door smoking his pipe, while Mama cut out school dresses for Sarai and Sophie on the dining room table and the children played hide-and-go seek outdoors (Bert was 'it'). Robby was standing by the chicken house door calling, "You can't find me, you can't find me," when Bert yelled out, "Look, there's someone with a lantern up on the Big Hill!"

Sophie whispered to Sarai, "He's just trying to get us to let on where we are."

But when they peeked out from their hiding place, sure enough, there was a light swinging back and forth up on top of the Big Hill. They ran to the house.

"Papa, Mama, come look. Someone is up on the Big Hill!"

Papa removed his pipe and stood up; Mama came out of the house, and they all stood together, speechless. Who could be up there? Hardly anyone ever came out to this remote farming country, and no one came out at night. The Big Hill was not private land. What could be going on?

They all watched for a while until Papa said, "Morning comes early. It's bedtime."

Everyone was so excited! Sophie and Sarai lay in bed whispering about who it could be and why they would be up there. They could hear whispering from Bert's and Robby's room and the low voices of Papa and Mama downstairs. Finally the house became quiet, with no sound but the wind and the distant 'whooo' of the night owl.

Everyone talked about it the next day until Papa said, "Forget it, it's no account. Let's get our work done."

Nevertheless, that night after Papa had climbed out of his barrel and gone into the house, the children ran up to the hill by the barn. Soon Mama came up, then they smelled Papa's pipe behind them. Sure enough, on the Big Hill in the distance a lantern began to swing back and forth, then a second lantern. Each person had a different opinion: Papa said it could be a bootlegger building a still; Mama thought someone digging for Indian artifacts; but Sophie, who wanted to write a mystery story, was sure it was someone either burying a body or digging one up.

The next night they waited but the lights didn't appear again.

"Mama," Sophie said as they did their chores, "I can't forget about the lights. I wish I knew what they were all about so I could write a story about them."

"I'd like to know too, so go get the other children and let's find out. Hurry before Papa gets home."

Mama was like an adventurous little girl sometimes. Papa probably wouldn't approve; it was lucky he'd had to go to a township meeting.

They all got in the old Model T while Mama and Bert took turns cranking, but it wouldn't start. Finally they pushed it up onto the little hill and coasted down till the motor turned over with a roar, then away they went down the road to the Big Hill. The old flivver had to be parked on another little hill off the road in case it wouldn't start again. The upward climb was a struggle through thick brush and wild roses, but Sophie was so excited she didn't notice her torn dress or scratched, bloody arms and legs. Finally they reached the summit, and stood gazing down into a long rectangular hole about seven or eight feet long, five feet wide and five feet deep. What could it be for? Who had invaded their countryside, who had dared to sneak in where everyone knew everyone else, cared for and supported each other, and everything was open and above-board? In silence Mama and the children walked back to the car. No one answered Robby as he repeated over and over, "A hole, a great big hole."

That night at supper they told Papa about what they had seen. He was sober.

"I had better find out if any of the neighbors saw anything, and we'll talk about it." Papa would take care of it. Sophie would remember it all her life and would write a story about it.

The end of the summer neared, Sarai and Sophie spent their days herding the cattle up on public land near the Big Hill. It had been a dry summer and the pasture grass was dried up. The cows were giving less milk each day; Sunday Biscuit's teats no longer dripped milk by milking time. Sarai and Sophie hated herding cattle; it was so hot. It was better after they found a shallow cave in the side of a hill where they could put their lunches and water jar, Sophie's doll and books, and Sarai's drawing paper and pencil. Sarai said she was too old to play with dolls, but condescended to dress them when there was 'nothing to do.' Some days even Goph got bored, and went home and refused to come back when they called him;

then sometimes the cows ran away if the girls got busy playing. They would be late getting them home and would be in trouble. Papa would say, "Go get a switch and bring it here to get a licking."

Once Sophie said, "But if we don't want to be spanked but you want to spank us, you should get the switch." She never tried that again!

Most days Goph stayed with the cattle. One afternoon they were all lying down in a hollow, with Goph nearby. "Let's explore a little," said Sarai. The two girls ran off through the underbrush. Never having had a plow or mower to it, the growth was high. The girls came over a little rise and saw a roof down below, sunken into the grass.

"Look," cried Sophie, "a haunted house!"

It was a small house with an attic above. They went through a sagging door, then stood still for a bit, shivering. It was quiet, with the sun shining through the dirty windows and no sign of anyone having lived there for a long time. In the peaceful silence they soon felt calm and eager to explore.

There was nothing much to find in the rooms downstairs but mouse droppings and old wasps' nest.

"Come on, Sarai, I dare you to go upstairs with me!"

They climbed the ladder and hesitated before they poked their noses through the trap door in the ceiling and looked around. Just a big bare space . . . but wait! Over in the corner was a big pile of paper. Intrigued, Sophie raised herself through the door and scurried across the floor.

"Come look, Sarai, old newspapers and catalogues, really old."

They sat and gazed at wonderful pictures of beautiful women dressed in clothing the like of which they had never seen before. There were Sears Roebuck catalogues, Montgomery Ward catalogues, and newspapers from many, many years ago.

All at once they heard a faint bark.

"Goph! The cows! What if a coyote is after them?"

Never had the girls run so fast, with visions of dead cattle and a bloody Goph valiantly trying to keep a whole pack of coyotes at bay. They fairly fell down the last little hill, only to find the cattle on their feet and starting for home with Goph behind them, looking back with frantic barks to signal the girls to get back to their jobs.

Sophie and Sarai never went back to the little old deserted house. Papa said, "No," and Mama, with a little smile on her lips, said, "Never while herding the cattle and never without me."

That night Sarai dreamed about being dressed up in one of those beautiful old gowns with a bustle fastened importantly behind, and a handsome beau bowing over her hand. Sophie dreamed about writing a story about a beautiful house and a body dug up from a lonely grave on top of a big hill.

4

Sophie was drying dishes, admiring the flowers on the plates. She could paint these, only she'd make the flowers a delicious blue. Sarai always finished washing the dishes long before Sophie finished drying them. She wiped slowly as she envisioned painting beautiful blue flowers on a canvas, and perhaps a lady wearing a bustle, admiring them.

"Sophie, come here."

Sarai was standing halfway down the stairs, whispering and gesturing.

"Look, Sophie. I'm getting a shape like Mama's, and Amy Johnson said that when you get breasts like this, then you have babies."

Sophie followed her upstairs.

"Oh, Sarai, you mustn't have babies yet. You want to go to high school next year, and you can't take a baby to high school."

"Well, Sophie, maybe Amy doesn't know everything! And anyway, a live baby would be more fun than your old dolls!"

Then Sophie had a horrible thought. Would she get a shape like Mama's and have a baby, and have to take it to high school, and not be able to be a dancer or an artist or a writer? She flung herself on the bed and began to sob loudly.

Mama's piano playing stopped. The girls heard her call, "Sarai, Sophie, come down please."

Sarai grabbed Sophie's hand and pulled her off the bed and down the stairs. Mama looked at Sophie's tear-stained face, and led them into the parlor. Hardly anyone went in there except Mama when she played the piano, or her whist club when they met, or relatives who came to visit. She sat down on the davenport and put a girl on each side of her.

"Now, tell me what's happening. Sisters shouldn't fight."

"We weren't fighting," said Sarai. "I was just showing her something about me and she started crying."

"Sophie, what made you cry?" asked Mama.

"Sarai showed me how she was getting shaped like you up here, and that meant she was having a baby; I'll get shaped like that too and I don't want to have a baby to take to high school. I want to study hard there and become a dancer or a painter or a writer." Sophie cried harder than ever. Mama was quiet for a minute as she hugged them both close to her, then she said, "As little girls grow to become women, they get shaped differently, and some day, after they go to high school and perhaps college, they may meet a nice man like Papa and love him, and he will love her; they will get married, and then it's time to have the baby."

Sophie sighed with relief.

"Then after I do all the things I want to do, I can get married, and maybe I can have my baby on a mattress under the trees the way Mrs. Johnson did."

Sophie didn't know why her Mama began laughing so hard that she jiggled the girls until they began to laugh too.

"We'd better see what we're going to have for supper.

It's almost time to bring in the cows for milking and Papa and the boys will be coming back from hauling rocks. Sarai, it's your turn to get the cows; Sophie, you need to peel potatoes and gather the boys."

* * *

Robby shook the hair off the old towel and threw it to Sophie yelling, "Your turn," as he ran outside sporting a 'rooster tail' that stuck straight up. Sophie took his place on the high stool, and Mama fastened a towel around her neck with a clothespin, snipped the barber shears a few times in the air, and started on her bangs.

"Please don't get them too short, Mama. I don't want to be teased."

Monday was a big day—the first day of school. Perhaps she wouldn't get teased this year since big old Al wouldn't be there. She hated him because he always smelled like cow manure and garlic. When she had a new haircut he always said, "That bowl your Mama put on your head when she cut your hair must have a chunk off the edge." Ha ha ha!

As Mama snipped away, Sophie thought about how much she loved school. When she had started first grade at five years of age, she could already read, write, and do numbers, so her teacher put her in second grade. She wondered what the teacher would be like this year. Papa was on the school board and had helped to hire her. It was hard to find a good teacher for a one-room school way out on the prairie. Papa said, "She's a big woman and she can whip the trousers off of you if you act up, Bert. But," he grinned, "she'll be pleased as punch when she hears how you and Sarai can read."

It was hard to go to sleep that night; would Monday ever come?

* * *

Sarai, Sophie and Bert ran down the road swinging their shiny syrup pails that held oatmeal cookies, apples, and sandwiches made of Mama's fresh bread. Mama had stayed up late Saturday night finishing new dresses for Sophie and Sarai and a new shirt for Bert. His bib overalls were new, stiff, and a little bit big. "Wait for me," he yelled as the girls ran ever faster to catch up with the Johnson kids ahead of them. The grass was still wet with dew and Sophie's new shoes and black stockings were getting wet; she squatted down to wipe her shoes with her petticoat, and raced on. The Johnson kids all had fresh haircuts and new clothes too.

Sophie thought, "You may have a bigger barn and a silo, but our Mama sews better clothes." Then she remembered Mama telling her, "You must never think bad thoughts about others," so she told Charity how pretty her dress was.

It was a two-and-one-half mile trip to school, part of the way on a graveled road, but soon they all left the road and cut across the pasture to make the distance shorter. Everyone was polite about holding down the barbed wire for each other. It would be terrible to get to school the very first day with their brand new clothes ripped. Ed Johnson, the oldest boy, went ahead to see if the resident herd of cattle was anywhere in sight. The bull had never really charged them, but sometimes he snorted and pawed the earth and Sophie's heart almost flew out of her mouth. "Come on," Ed yelled and they all pounded over the little hill, down the other side, around through the fence, and there was the little schoolhouse with its flag flying above it, waiting to welcome them.

*   *   *

The first day of school was over. Sophie, the Johnsons, Bert, and Sarai were on their way home. Each had left part of a sandwich or cookie in the lunch pails to snack on. Bert said, "I'm tired and I don't think our new teacher, Miss Grimm, likes me."

"Well," said Sophie, "you were pulling that new girl's hair."

A new family had moved into the area. They were from a large town where the school taught physical education, and at recess they did cartwheels and stood on their hands to show how much better their old school was. Sarai said, "They're just showoffs, and I don't think they should have been showing their bloomers." Charity Johnson whispered that they had had on orange bloomers. Imagine!

"We shouldn't be talking about bloomers in front of boys!"

Bert came up behind Sarai and began yelling, "Bloomers, bloomers, bloomers, orange bloomers, orange bloomers!"

Sophie put her hand over his mouth and said sternly, "We'd better hurry or we'll be in trouble."

They had come home the long way, and it was getting late. Sarai began running.

"Remember, Mama said after we got our clothes changed, we had to go out to the pasture and pick up cow chips."

Sophie hated picking up cow chips but knew that Mama would need a lot to burn in the kitchen range, since they would be home all day tomorrow. She remembered the time she picked up one that was soft in the middle. She had run to the windmill and pumped water over her hand and scrubbed and scrubbed, but later she had thought about it and couldn't eat the big warm slice of bread Mama handed to her.

As they lay in bed that night, Sarai and Sophie talked about school. There were twenty pupils altogether, enough to have good games of run, sheep, run, and ante-I-over. Sarai thought that one of the new boys liked her, but Sophie just thought of the new geography book with its pictures, how well she could read it, and how proud she felt when Miss Grimm asked her to write a problem on the board.

5

The whole family was gathered around the table with the Sears Roebuck and Montgomery Ward catalogues open in front of them.

"Now, no quarreling," said Mama. "First we'll pick out shoes and stockings, underwear, scarves, mittens, and stocking caps. I need to order dried fruit, beans, lentils, oatmeal, coffee, tea, and . . . let's see; I have my list somewhere here. Oh, and Papa needs a new sheepskin coat. Then you children may look at toys."

Sophie had seen a picture of some 'Roman boots' in the catalogue. Oh, if only Papa would say "yes" to those. Papa drew an outline of each child's foot on a piece of wrapping paper to be put in with the order. When it was Sophie's turn, she looked up beseechingly and said, "Papa, could I have these?"

She showed him the picture of the boots in the catalogue.

"It's up to your mother."

"Sophie, those are just dress-up shoes. You need school shoes."

"Please, Mama; Sarai's school shoes are too small for her and they're still not worn out. I'll wear those if you'll let me have these. Please, Mama!"

"Well," Mama said, "I guess you'll need them for the Christmas program. Sarai, what kind of dress-up shoes do you want? You'll also need new everyday shoes. Bert's shoes are already too small, but too big for Robby. Oh dear, it's a good thing we had a good wheat crop this year."

Mama finished the large order and Sarai, Sophie, Bert, and Robby pored over the toy sections. They knew they wouldn't get everything they wanted, but each wrote his or her name beside the thing he wanted most for Christmas. It was fun to dream, anyway. Sophie waited until Bert and Robby were looking at the picture of an erector set and Sarai had gone to get a drink. She turned to the doll section and gazed at the sweet face of a baby doll dressed in a long gown, wrapped in a blanket. Sarai would laugh and say, "A doll? What a baby you are."

Sophie didn't care, she wanted that doll. "Mama?" She slipped behind her mother as she checked her long order, and whispered in her ear, "I'm just going to put an X on what I want."

Mama looked at her, smiled, then reached up and patted her face and said, "I love you."

On the way to school the next morning, they took turns carrying the important letter with the orders in it to the mailbox by the gravel road. Now they'd count the days until big packages started to arrive, winter clothes could be tried on, food stored, and Sophie would have her new Roman boots.

"Brr, I'm freezing," said Bert as he put the letters in the mailbox. "I'll be glad when we get our new mittens and caps."

Sophie looked down at her overshoes. Mama said they had better wear them as it looked like snow. Sophie didn't want to, for fear she'd get a hole in one of them; then when she wore her new Roman boots to the Christmas program, the snow might get inside her overshoes onto the beautiful boots. Maybe it wouldn't snow for

Christmas! But there always was snow for Christmas, heaps of it. No, she didn't want the ground to be bare for Christmas. There had to be snow! She'd just put wadded newspaper in the toes of the overshoes.

She ran on to catch up with the other children with her scarf blowing out behind, singing "Jingle Bells" as she thought about Christmas and the doll she'd ordered from Santa. Papa and Mama always laughed when the children picked out the gifts they yearned for in the catalogue and mailed the order—and then talked about Santa bringing the gifts! But it was all part of the fun, and just maybe . . .

The wind was blowing harder as they ran up the school steps. Bert said smartly, "I'll see how cold it is."

He stuck his tongue on the long brass handle of the door and let out a shriek. His tongue had stuck to the icy handle and pulled off some skin. Miss Grimm came to the door and led the crying boy into the cloak hall. She put a cold wet cloth on his tongue and patted his head gently. Bert looked up at her through tear-filled eyes and knew, finally, that she had become a good friend.

Sophie was engrossed in her geography book, especially the parts about England and Norway, the countries from which her ancestors had come. Perhaps someday she'd be able to go to those places and see where her ancestors had lived. She became aware of brightness in the room, a soft 'plop, plop' against the windows, and looked up. White flakes were hitting the window softly, sliding down, coming faster and faster. Someone called out, "Miss Grimm, Miss Grimm."

Miss Grimm turned from the chalkboard.

"Children, we don't . . ."

Then she saw the snow, smiled and followed the children as they all rushed to the windows to watch the first snow fall.

"Miss Grimm, may we have recess soon?"

"Get all your wraps on now and we'll go out. When we come back in, we'll discuss what causes it to snow and what snow is made of."

Soon everyone was bundled up and out the door. Snowflakes were flying, and everyone compared the snowflakes that lay like delicate lace doilies on their sleeves and mittens. Sophie and Laura Riekler went out by the barn, away from the flying snowballs, and made angels in the snow. As Sophie lay on her back fanning her arms and legs out wider and wider to make the shape of wings, she wondered if there really were angels looking down and smiling at them. *Perhaps an angel will tell God how very much I want the Roman boots and the doll,* she thought. *I'm really afraid to pray for them, because He might think I'm selfish. Perhaps if I pray that Bert's tongue will stop hurting then God will want me to have at least my boots.* She got up, looked at her beautiful snow angel, and realized that Miss Grimm was calling them in.

The snow kept coming down, so Sophie wasn't surprised when the schoolhouse door flew open and Papa came in stomping the snow off of his overshoes and shaking it off his old sheepskin-lined coat and cap. His face was red and his eyebrows were frozen white. He boomed out, "Miss Grimm, I'm taking my kids and the Johnson kids home if that's all right with you."

Sophie and the others put on their outdoor clothes again, grabbed their lunch pails as they shouted good-bye, and all piled into Papa's sleigh. Mama had put in hot salt bags and quilts over the straw, but Papa said, "Your mother babies you too much! Get out and run. Get your circulation going."

Finally Papa told them to get in the sleigh. They snuggled under the covers, opened their lunch pails and ate with snowflakes falling on their sandwiches and cookies. Miss Grimm didn't let them trade food in school, but now Sophie was able to trade her oatmeal cookies to Charity for molasses ones.

At their front gate the Johnson kids jumped out, dumping the snow on top of the quilts into the other children's laps, and Papa waited and watched through the falling snow until they reached their kitchen door. The horses wanted to get home. The bells on their harnesses jingled merrily as they broke back into a trot. How nice it was of Papa to stop by the house and let Sarai and Sophie out, before Papa and Bert went on to the barn to put the tired horses in. Mama opened the door and helped them off with their coats and caps, shaking out the snow in the lean-to where they left their overshoes.

How good it was to be home, safe and warm. The kitchen cook stove was red-hot, a teakettle was sending up clouds of steam, fresh bread was cooling on the counter and six mugs sat on the kitchen table.

"Hot cocoa and fresh bread!" shouted Sophie as she did a mad whirl in the middle of the linoleum-covered kitchen floor. She almost forgot that she had eaten her 'dinner' on the way home. Robby sat at the dining room table cutting out pictures of toys from the old Montgomery Ward catalogue and pasting them, with the flour and water Mama had mixed up, into a scrapbook made of brown wrapping paper tied together with string. He waved his book and yelled, "See my pretty book!" Then, "I'm hungry."

Sophie wiped the paste off his nose, kissed him and said, "You did a good job, Robby. Are you going to get ALL these toys for Christmas?"

Mama gave Sophie a warning glance.

"Remember, Robby, just one with your name on it. Santa can't carry that many toys."

"I put my name on it, see?" cried Robby. There, above a red car, was a big "r-o-d-d-y."

"Papa hasn't had dinner yet," said Mama. "So we'll all sit down with him and have our bread and cocoa. When we get through, we get a surprise."

"I know what it is," Sarai said. "But I won't tell."

"You're mean, Sarai," cried Bert. "Then I'll just beat you at a game of carrom!" Carrom! A perfect day to play their favorite indoor game.

They all folded their hands for the blessing, quickly drank their cocoa, cleared the dishes away, and then Papa said, "Come on, Bert. I need your help."

The other children heard Bert's shout of joy from the parlor. Papa and he pushed back the old quilt hanging in the doorway to the parlor and came in, carrying huge boxes. The catalogue order had come! Everyone began to talk at once and rush around the table to open the boxes, but Mama said, "Let's just sit until Papa and I have opened the boxes; then Sarai and Sophie, you may distribute everything."

"Me too, me too," piped up Robby.

Out came new caps, mittens, mufflers, shoes, and Papa's new sheepskin coat; Mama's new dress-up dress; material for new Christmas dresses for Sophie and Sarai; new shirts for Bert and Robby; raisins, dried prunes, coffee, rice, oatmeal . . . The list went on and on. Everyone had to help stack the groceries on the table. What a flurry and hustle-bustle then, as the new clothes were unwrapped and tried on. Sophie could hardly wait to get her boots. Finally, near the bottom of the crate, there was the box, with a picture of a beautiful pair of Roman boots on the outside. She grabbed it and ran up the stairs to her bedroom. Hugging the box to her chest, she frantically tugged on the laces of her old shoes. Would they never come off? Sophie took the new boots out of the box, handling them as if they were made of glass, then tried to push her foot into a boot.

"These darn old stockings. They're just too thick."

She went to the dresser and found a pair of summer knee socks. These would do. After much tugging she got both boots on and stood up. Oh, but they were tight! Her toes felt as if they were bent double and the fancy laces wouldn't come together over her chubby legs. She walked back and forth until her feet felt numb, then stumbled down the stairs. Trying to smile, she said, "Aren't they beautiful and they fit perfectly!"

Mama looked at her face and then down at her feet and said, "Sophie, we can send them back and get a bigger size."

Sophie panicked. They'd never get here in time for the Christmas Program.

"No, please, Mama, they fit just fine."

She tramped valiantly up the stairs, limped through Bert and Robby's room to the room she shared with Sarai, tugged off the most beautiful boots in the world, threw herself on the bed and sobbed and sobbed. Suddenly she stopped and sat up. She had just remembered something she had learned when studying about China. The Chinese ladies prided themselves on having small feet, and bound their feet tightly so they would stay tiny. At least her feet wouldn't grow any more before the Christmas Program. Satisfied, Sophie placed her new boots in the box, sat them carefully by her side of the bed so she could look at them the first thing in the morning, and started downstairs to see what else might emerge from those big boxes.

Bert called up through the register that let up heat from the dining room.

"Hurry down, Sophie, we're going to play carrom."

When it started to get cold in the fall Mama always fastened a big old patchwork quilt in the doorway between the parlor and the dining room. The big floor register that brought the heat up from the cellar furnace was right in that doorway between the two rooms. Since the parlor wasn't used much in the cold winter weather, Mama closed it off by setting chairs to hold the edge of the quilt down on the parlor side of the doorway, so that all of the heat went into the dining room. Sometimes Sophie peeked around the edge of the quilt and thought how lonesome and neglected everything looked in there; Mama's piano, the big revolving bookcase with all of Mama's books from her days of teaching school, the stiff parlor chairs, the desk with Papa's important papers inside, and the library table with the black and white photographs of Grandpa and Grandma Putnam on top and old tintypes in the drawers. Sophie always wondered why they all sat so stiff and straight in those pictures, looking miserable. Life must not have been much fun in those days. Even the old phonograph that stood in the corner looked as if it would never play again.

Bert put the carrom board on a kitchen stool and placed it over the middle of the big heat register. He and Sarai were already sitting on chairs around it, swinging their legs in the warm air. Sophie pulled up a chair, almost knocking the carrom board off the stool. Just then Robby came running into the room yelling, "Me play, me play!"

"Oh, no!" groaned Bert, Sarai and Sophie in unison.

Papa looked over his glasses. Then he took Robby on his lap and showed him the pictures in the newspaper,

The Minneapolis Tribune, that he was reading. Papa didn't believe in reading fairy tales to children.

"You children need to learn about facts, what's going on in the world."

Sophie loved to play carrom. She wasn't good at shooting the red rings with the stick, so she snapped them with her finger and thumb into the pockets. Sometimes a ring went flying down through the heat register into the furnace. Hopefully it fell in between the fire pot and the jacket that surrounded it rather than into the fire. Then someone would bribe Robby to crawl in and get the ring, since he was the only one small enough to fit. If the furnace was too hot, they would have to wait until summer to retrieve it. Many a carrom game was played with only half the rings.

Sarai put down her carrom stick and said, "Just think. No picking up cow chips, herding cattle or weeding potatoes for a while. . . . I love winter."

Papa had set Robby down and was reading the paper. He suddenly smacked the paper down on the table, muttering to himself. "This country is going to hell in a handbasket," then fixed Sarai with a stern look.

"Girl, we need to work the year around to keep the family going. There is still coal to be hauled from the cellar to keep your mother's range hot, potatoes to be sprouted, milking to be done, calves to feed, snow to shovel and if you don't remember to bring up lignite to keep the cook stove banked all night, you'll be hauling cow chips from the granary to start new fires every morning. It's about time your mother taught you girls to sew and cook. Bert and I will be cleaning and oiling harnesses. There'll be no idle hands around here. And Robby . . ."

He looked down at Robby who was running his little

iron car back and forth over Goph's back while Goph grunted a bit and continued to sleep.

"Robby will just spend his time growing."

That was one of the longest speeches Sophie had ever heard Papa make. Her mind wasn't on carrom anymore. She thought about growing up, going to high school, getting married, having children and how much work there would always be to do. She thought about her precious Roman boots. Mama wouldn't like to have her tear up a towel for strips to wrap her feet in, so she had decided against that idea. But what if she 'grew up' so much by the time of the Christmas program that she wouldn't be able to get the boots on and stand up in front of everybody and recite her piece in the program....

Suddenly she realized that Mama was calling from the kitchen, "Time to put away the carrom board and set the table. Pork chops and white gravy!"

There was a mad scramble and soon everyone was at the table, eating ravenously. Sophie looked around at her family. Everything looked so normal, so 'usual.' She saw Bert slipping his crusts onto the little shelf on the underside of the table for Goph to find and devour. Sarai was picking at her food and saying "No" to Mama's wonderful bread pudding (so she wouldn't get fat). Robby was rubbing his spoon, smeared with gravy, in his hair. Papa was glancing sternly around to check table manners, while Mama gave a little warning shake of her head and a smile when she saw Bert stuff his bread into his mouth before Papa noticed that the crusts were missing. *I don't think I want to grow up,* thought Sophie. *I want everything to stay just like now—even if I do have to pick up cow chips, weed potatoes and herd the cows.*

*   *   *

The Christmas toys ordered from 'Santa Claus' had not yet arrived in the mail. Sophie kept close watch to see if Papa slipped packages into the cold, closed-up parlor. After he came back from trips to town, Papa and Mama went around talking in low tones, then said things like: "Won't it be fun going to Grandpa's and Grandma's this Christmas?"

Last year before Christmas Papa and Mama had had a little disagreement with Grandpa and Grandma, and Christmas had been spent at home. Sophie tried to remember what it was all about. Papa and Grandpa had argued about whose wheat had yielded the best and then Grandma asked Mama why she didn't put eggshells in her coffee. What silly things to spoil Christmas with.

Sophie had vivid memories of other Christmases at Grandma's house. How much fun it was to be tucked into the big sleigh with Bert, Sarai, Robby and all of the mysterious wrapped presents, under thick quilts with hot stones or salt bags for their feet. Papa in his sheepskin coat looked like a big bear sitting on the spring seat up front, and Mama, sitting next to him bundled in her own quilt, with her fur collar pulled up around her face and her cap pulled down, looked like a pretty, frosty doll. It always seemed as if they would never get to their destination. Sometimes Papa had the children get out and run beside the sleigh, puffing, with their cheeks turning red from the exertion of wading through the snowbanks in their heavy overshoes and cumbersome coats. Then back into the sleigh and under the quilts, only to find that the salt bags had turned cold and the snow from their overshoes rubbed off on the quilts. Just in time, Grandpa's farm would come into view.

Aunt Tillie would be waving from the frost-covered window where she had been scratching ice pictures as she waited impatiently. She was not much older than Sarai and oh, what fun they always had, giggling and sharing secrets. Then the door opened and Grandma would appear, rubbing her hands on her spotless white apron, ready to give everyone a big hug. Grandpa stayed put in his Morris chair in the dining room, smoking his pipe, and greeted them with his slow smile, acting surprised as if he hadn't known they were coming.

"Well, well, look what Boots dragged in." Boots was the old sheep dog who spent most of his time lying by Grandpa's chair.

Sophie loved Grandpa and Grandma's house. Everything about it was spotless, just like Grandma's apron. When Grandma walked around, straightening a pillow here, a braided rug there, her apron crackled and she laughed and talked, all at the same time. She was Mama's stepmother and only fourteen years older. Sometimes they argued like sisters. Grandma said that coffee wasn't coffee without egg shells to "clear it." Mama said, "Not in my kitchen."

Mama sewed beautifully, but Grandma said, "I never had the knack and I never will."

Anyway, Christmas was great fun. They always stayed overnight, although Papa grumbled and maintained, in a loud voice, that "Son of a—" "Sunday Biscuit!" Mama quickly filled in for him—needed to be milked on time. Neighbor Johnson probably wouldn't get around to milking her before noon.

Aunt Tillie would take Sarai and Sophie to her bedroom where they whispered together about what they thought they were getting for Christmas. When Aunt Tillie and Sarai started giggling about boys Sophie would go find a book to read. Grandma always had a regular feast prepared, and after dinner she would open up the cold parlor and call Grandpa to start a fire in the potbellied stove. Sophie could never forget how the Christmas tree looked, standing over in the corner by the organ, with a shiny star on top and red candles in little tin holders clipped on the branches. It was just waiting for the popcorn garlands that the children made to string on the branches, and for the candles to be lit, casting a radiant glow over the entire room. Everyone would sit down and wait for Santa to come striding into the parlor with a big bag and a "Ho, ho, ho!" For some reason, Santa's "Ho, ho, hos" always sounded like Uncle Ralph, who (Grandpa said with a wink) had had to go to the neighbors for something. Next came the opening of gifts, the wrapping paper flying around amidst all the "Oohs" and "Ahs," and then it was time for Grandma to sit at the organ and play "Away in a Manger" as everyone sang.

It was hard to sleep on Christmas night, but somehow they always managed. One year Aunt Tillie got a new sled, and all the next day the children slid down the hill above the barn until Uncle Ralph called them in to eat supper before Papa hitched up the horses and they headed for home. It seemed to Sophie that the homemade fudge, ribbon candy, left-over goose, plum pudding and Grandma's special rolls tasted better every year. All too soon it would be time to pile in the sled under the quilts that Grandma had warmed for them, wave goodbye with a "Merry Christmas and Happy New Year," and, with the clip-clop of the horse's hooves and the sleigh bells ringing in their ears, drop off to sleep. Sophie always tried to stay awake the longest so that she could think about how much fun they had had. Each year she told herself, "This is the very best Christmas yet, and next year I want it to be better!"

* * *

It was the week before Christmas. Mama had just finished cutting the children's hair. She had to do an especially good job as tomorrow night was the Christmas Program at school. Oh dear, there was still so much to do. There were Sarai's and Sophie's dresses still to be hemmed, buttons to be sewed on Bert's new shirt, and cake to be baked for refreshments. Mama decided to bake what she called the 'War Cake,' a recipe that used no eggs, milk, or butter. It was filled with raisins and with a nice frosting it would be fine. She was short on eggs these days, as the hens always quit laying during the cold winter. When Sophie went out to see if there were any eggs she would come back saying, "Those old hens are pouting again, Mama."

Mama loved watching the Christmas program. She and the other mothers always brought bed sheets to string up on wires across the end of the school room, to form a stage and dressing rooms, and how ashamed she would be if her sheets weren't as white as those of the other mothers'. She had left the bed sheets out on the line all last night, to freeze and whiten, and they looked beautiful! Dingy sheets mustn't keep her heart from bursting with pride when Sarai came out to sing "Away in a Manger." Sophie spoke her piece, and Bert, as Joseph, bowed over the Christ Child in the manger.

"Bert, bring in the wash tub," Mama called.

Baths were taken in front of the kitchen range, with much shivering and giggling then it was off to their rooms to put on their finery. Hair was combed and slicked down with a last glance in the wavy old mirror on the dresser in the girls' room, then coats, caps, mufflers and overshoes were hurried into and everyone tumbled into the big sleigh. Friday night had finally come! It was a cold, clear night; the moon was a huge, orange ball in the sky. The horses' hooves made a crunching sound in the snow and the bells on their harnesses tinkled merrily. The children sang "Jingle Bells," then grew silent as each repeated their parts in the program to themselves. Sophie tried to sing loudly and to remember the piece she was going to speak, but all she could think of was how her feet hurt in those beautiful, too-tight Roman boots!

Gas lamps sent a cherry glow out through the big schoolhouse windows, onto the proud parents and their suddenly shy children filing in the door, all dressed in their finest. Soon the program was ready to begin. The sheets-turned-curtains swept dramatically open to the sight of Mother Mary, Joseph, and the Baby Jesus lying in the manger. Robby had been invited to be the Baby Jesus, as there didn't seem to be either a large doll in the neighborhood or a small baby. Mama and Papa had cautioned him to lie quietly and not pull the covers off to reveal a very large baby, but Robby was too excited about being so important, and as soon as the curtains opened he sat up waving his chubby little hand, yelling, "Mama and Papa, see me up here!"

"Joseph" hurriedly tried to get the curtain pulled but one sheet caught on the wire.

"Oh, not my best sheet, please!" whispered Mama to Papa.

"Joseph" finally got the curtain closed, then stuck his head out, a big grin on his face. Miss Grimm appeared from behind the sheet, her face flushed and announced, "I'm sorry for the little, er, uh . . . The program will now begin."

When Sarai came out in her pretty new dress and sang so sweetly, Mama forgot her sheet. *Oh, well, if it was torn, it's Christmas-time . . .* she thought, *. . . and any-*

way, I couldn't tell if it was my sheet or not. I guess everyone froze their sheets—they're all white. Sophie knew she was next, to "Speak her Piece." How could she ever walk out there without limping, in those precious, beautiful, oh so tight Roman boots? But now here she was, standing oh so straight, her hands clenched at her sides.

"What can I give Him, poor as I am? If I were a Shepherd, I'd give Him a lamb. If I were a Wise Man, I'd do my part. But what can I give Him? I'll give Him my heart." Her breath came in a sob as she stumbled back behind the curtain-sheets. Now she could take off her boots, hide them under her coat, and sit down on the floor with her head on her arms, tears trickling down the front of her new silk-pongee dress.

The program was over and Sophie could hear everyone talking and laughing and knew they were eating her favorite kind of cake, the kind that Mama had brought, but she didn't care. Papa found her there. He didn't say a word but just led her out to a chair and brought her a plate of food. Mama sat down and put her arm around her.

"My sweet girl, you said your piece so well. It sounded as if it came right from your heart."

Everyone was getting wraps on and talking about how good the program had been. "Merry Christmas" filled the air, and Sophie hoped that no one noticed when Papa picked her up and carried her to the sled. He tucked the quilt around her, then pulled her boots out of his pocket and pushed them down beside her. The next thing she knew they were home and Papa was carrying her into the house. The Roman boots were never seen again, but the next order to Sears Roebuck included a pair of shiny patent leather slippers and a drawing of Sophie's foot, with two inches to spare.

6

Sophie woke up and started to climb out of bed but fell back with a thump. Oh, she felt terrible!—so dizzy and weak, her face was itching and hot and her eyes hurt.

"Sarai," she moaned, "please call Mama. Please." Sarai took one look at Sophie, then went racing down the stairs.

"Mama, Mama," she called, "Sophie's face is all red and puffy."

Mama came up, took one look and said, "Measles, and it's almost Christmas!"

She pulled the dark green window shade down and brought Sophie a big glass of water.

"Do you feel like eating? How about some 'sick food'?"

'Sick food' was always milk toast: crisp hot toast topped with melted butter and hot milk. Sophie just mumbled "No," and buried her head in the pillow.

It seemed days before she felt good again, and by then it was Sarai's turn to be sick in bed, then Bert and Robby took their turns. Sophie heard Mama say to Papa, "Christmas won't be Christmas this year. The Christmas toys haven't come, the children with measles, and we won't even be able to get to the folks this year."

"Well," Papa said as he gazed out the window, "it looks like more snow is on its way. We'll probably be snowed in, anyway."

Sure enough, two days before Christmas it began to

snow—and snow and snow and snow! Papa, Mr. Johnson and the Johnson boys hitched up the horses to their sleds and laboriously plowed through the snowbanks to town. It was almost dark when Papa got home. The milking was done, Sophie had checked for eggs and the animals were all fed. It had been difficult and so cold, digging paths to the barn and chicken house and pulling the heavy 'Papa-made' sled to the barn with the cream can and milk pails. But Sophie, Sarai and Bert forgot the cold as they waited for Papa and talked excitedly about what had happened that afternoon.

They had taken their roller skates as they trudged their way to the barn with the heavy sled, and climbed to the hayloft. There they pushed the hay back, leaving the center of the floor bare, then fastened their roller skates onto their overshoes and tried to skate over the rough, uneven floor boards. Robby had insisted on coming along, so they wrapped him up so that only his big blue eyes showed, and sat him on the sled ahead of the cream can and pails. He crowed with delight, waved his red mittens in the air and shouted, "Go faster, go faster."

It was so good to get out after days of red spots and coughing. Robby was plopped down in the hay to watch them try to skate on the rough boards. All at once he disappeared and they heard a cry from below. "Don't eat my new mitten!"

Sophie, heart pounding, ran out of the haymow door and plowed her way through the snow around the barn and into the door at the back. The cows in their stanchions were moving and shifting around as if they had been disturbed from their peaceful cud-chewing. Sophie heard Robby say, "Bad cow! Give me my mitten."

Sure enough, there was Robby in the hay manger in front of Sunday Biscuit, and Sunday Biscuit was chewing vigorously on the red mitten. Robby had fallen down the hole that was used to throw the hay down to the cows.

Sophie pushed carefully past her old enemy, snatched away the red mitten—which the old lady surrendered reluctantly—and gathered Robby up in her arms. She stood there for a moment, holding him closely as he sniffled on her shoulder. Then she had a lovely thought. "This is almost like the first Christmas; a manger full of hay, a baby (though a big one) in the manger, cows chewing their cuds. Only I don't think any cows were chewing on a red mitten. Now if only we had angels singing and a bright star!" Lo and behold: when she went outside she saw that it had grown dark, and there was a star glowing right where it belonged.

It was time to get the milking done. Sophie took Robby back to the house, listened for a minute as he told Mama his hair-raising tale about the huge monster who dragged him down in a dark cellar and ate his red mitten, then went back to the barn. Sarai, Sophie and Bert grabbed their little stools and a milk pail each, ready to sit down to squeeze the warm milk from the dripping teats.

"Bert," Sophie asked, "would you please milk Sunday Biscuit? She'll probably remember that I took the red mitten from her and kick my pail over."

It was fun to sit there with one's head against the cow's flank, listening to the rat-a-tat of the milk as it was squeezed from the cow's bags into the pails. The mother cat sat close by, waiting for Sophie to send a stream of warm milk into her mouth. When the chores were done, they slogged back to the house to wait for Papa. The moment they heard him stomping the snow from his overshoes out in the lean-to, everyone ran to open the door, all shouting at once: "Did you remember cranberries? Mama said we can string them tonight. Oh, and what about the oysters—and was there any good mail?"

Everyone knew what 'good mail' meant. Papa turned up his earflaps and took off his cap, then put the wooden box of oysters, the cranberries, the sacks of ribbon candy and the chocolate drops on the kitchen counter, and a huge bag of mail on the dining room table. But no mysterious packages from Sears Roebuck and Montgomery Ward.

"Well," Papa said, "it's beginning to look like Christmas around here."

"Not without our presents," Sophie muttered quietly, then felt her face turn red from having such mean, selfish thoughts.

Mama, Sarai, and Sophie hurried to finish fixing supper while Papa sat down to devour the huge pile of *The Minneapolis Tribune*. How he'd missed reading the newspaper when the mail hadn't come. He was tired. It had been a hard twenty miles to town and back in the swirling snow and the harsh, cold wind.

Out in the lean-to Bert turned the handle of the cream separator, then took the warm skim milk out to the barn to feed to the calves and to the mother cat with her new kittens, snuggled up in the calf manger. Goph was playing out in the snowbanks and almost got his short legs stuck in a especially big drift. He whined at the kitchen door until Mama let him in. With a big shake he sent a shower of snow all over the kitchen floor, then skittered into the dining room to hide under the table, where he would wait for the crusts of bread that Bert sneaked onto the little shelf under the table for him.

Finally supper was over. Bert said, "No dessert, Mama? Please don't say, 'Run down and get a jar of peaches.' I'm tired of peaches."

Mama smiled and went back into the kitchen. She came back with six bowls on a serving tray, and in each bowl was a big scoop of rich, whipped cream that smelled of vanilla. The children looked out the window. A fresh mantle of snow had just fallen, leaving the whole outdoors glistening pure white in the moonlight.

"Snow ice cream, snow ice cream," they chorused.

They rushed into their coats, caps, mufflers and overshoes and out they went, carrying their bowls and gazing in awe at the beautiful white world. Mama set the kerosene lamp in the dining room window so they could see to heap the fresh, clean snow on top of the whipped cream in the bowls and then stir, stir, stir. What a smacking of lips as they pulled out the spoons they had shoved in their pockets, and began to devour everyone's favorite dessert. Mama came out with two big bowls for Papa and her, and everyone laughed as she tried to fill two bowls at once.

* * *

Christmas Eve came. Mama took down the quilt from between the parlor and the dining room, so that the parlor would get warm and cozy. Sophie was the first child into the room. She just stood and gazed and gazed. How beautiful the little artificial tree from Montgomery Ward looked, with the garland of red and green twisted paper, cardboard angels, Santas and animals all covered with glitter and hung with tinsel, and the popcorn and cranberries strung on cords and draped on the branches. Then there were the red candles, ready to be lit, in the shiny tin holders snapped onto each twig. In the dining room, the table was set with Mama's best dishes. Her prized hot-chocolate set of six delicate china cups and the tall, beautiful carnation-trimmed pitcher held the place of honor in the center. On Christmas Day there would be turkey or goose, sage dressing, creamed onions, turnips and rutabagas, dill and Million Dollar pickles, fruit cake and steamed pudding; but Christmas Eve wouldn't be Christmas Eve without oyster stew!

After they had savored the milky, buttery stew, the table was cleared of everything but the chocolate pitcher and cups, and everyone went into the parlor. Mama sat down at the piano and played "Star of the East." Papa sat in his old leather Morris chair with Robby on his lap. Sarai, Bert and Sophie sat on the floor with their feet on the heat register, and listened. All at once Mama swung into "Jingle Bells," and the children jumped up and began to sing and dance around the beautiful little Christmas tree, while the candles on the tree twinkled merrily and even the angel on top seemed to nod approvingly. They danced and danced until Robby got so dizzy spinning around that he fell in a heap on the floor. Then Mama went back to playing, "Star of the East," very softly, and when she finished they all went outside to look for the star, without even thinking how cold it was.

As they sat in silence at the table drinking delicious cocoa topped with big gobs of whipped cream, out of those delicate little cups, Sophie thought, *I wonder if it felt like this when the Baby was born in the manger, after the angels sang and it was oh so quiet . . . and here we are, quietly drinking our cocoa. Is everyone thinking about the Baby in the manger?* She smiled at Mama and Mama smiled back, as if to say "I know what you're thinking about. I am too."

*   *   *

"Sarai," whispered Sophie, as she cuddled up to her

sister's warm back, "do you think that Santa will come even though there were no packages in the mail?"

"Of course. Papa and Mama will see to it."

*   *   *

Papa's voice roared up through the register.

"Merry Christmas!"

Sophie and Sarai jumped out of bed, put on their slippers and raced downstairs after Bert who was sliding down the banister holding Robby in front of him. Robby was rubbing his eyes and chirping, "Santa's come, Santa's come."

Bert looked at the beautiful, handmade wooden Model T car, complete with a garage, under the tree, then looked at Papa. Papa's eyes were twinkling. Robby hugged his new stocking doll, wrapped himself in the little blanket that was made of the same flannel as his pajamas and started up the stairs, saying, "We go beddy-bye."

Sarai and Sophie put on their new white aprons and mob caps, brandishing their little brooms just daring dirt to come their way. Mama had made the brooms by cutting the handles of old brooms shorter and trimming and retying the cane. She didn't realize how big the girls had grown, and that they used the big broom very well.

"Don't say anything, Sophie," whispered Sarai. "Let's remember to use these, now."

The stockings were emptied, next, of oranges (wherever had Mama kept them hidden?), fudge, ribbon candy, chocolate drops, oatmeal cookies and a "Promise Letter" in the toes, for the catalogue gifts that would come later. Everyone had new crocheted or knitted sweaters, and Papa had a new 'Made by Mama' shirt!

The children then ran and got the gifts they had

made for Mama: a vase, made from a quart jar with pretty stones and seashell macaroni glued on; a picture made by painting a silhouette on a piece of a window pane that was broken when Bert hit a baseball through the dining room window; a frame for the picture made of cardboard decorated with macaroni and old beads; and from Robby, a picture he had drawn of Goph chasing Sunday Biscuit. Oh, and for Papa the children had made a story-book, by pasting pictures from old newspapers on folded brown wrapping paper, with something that each had learned in school written below each picture. A piece of twine tied the book together.

"But where is Mama's gift from Papa?" whispered Bert.

In fact, Papa seemed to have disappeared. Suddenly the front door opened and Papa, a huge grin spreading over his face, came in carrying a big, long package wrapped in grocer's paper, which he plopped in Mama's lap. She let out a squeal because it was so cold, then removed the paper—and there was a big, frozen fish fresh from a Minnesota lake. For a minute Mama looked frozen herself. Then she jumped up and gave Papa a great big hug as she said, "How did you know I was hungering for fresh fish? It's the best gift you've ever given me!"

". . . almost!" Sophie heard her mutter under her breath, as she bustled into the kitchen. She returned with a platter of cinnamon rolls, followed by an omelet smelling of bacon and onions.

That night, as Sophie crawled into bed, her stomach feeling as if it were about to burst, her precious new Christmas gifts placed carefully on a chair, she yawned hugely and announced to the world in general, THIS was the best Christmas ever!

* * *

Finally the magical day came. The snow had quit falling and lay in huge, windswept banks against the buildings. All of the neighbors had brought their shovels and made the roads into town passable. Papa set off in the big old sleigh to take in cans and cans of cream as well as crocks of Mama's butter to trade for groceries. Mr. Johnson and his boys came snorting up in their Model T, the engine loudly protesting about having to work its way to town, but Papa said, "Darn fools. I know my team will make it."

Mama came running out to yell at Papa, waving the long grocery list in the frosty air. Papa stopped the eager horses as Bert ran over to hand him the list. He stored it safely in the pocket of his old sheepskin coat, yelled "Giddiup" to his horses, slapped the reins over their steaming backs and was off.

Surely the long-awaited packages would come. The children took turns at the dining room window, scratching off the frost to make pictures of mountains and roads, watching for Papa to get home. It would be a long wait, as he had to pick up the mail and get a load of lignite for the furnace, as well as get the groceries.

Sophie went upstairs to look once more at the bed she had made for her new doll. She had used an old, oval grape basket that should be just the right size. Mama had given her a piece of white flannel and she hemmed the edges with blue thread. It didn't look much like Mama's sewing, but her 'new baby' wouldn't care. She had even made a pillow stuffed with rags, and a tiny pillowcase. Sophie put the basket on the end of her bed and went to the window. She drew her breath in sharply. The frost had formed castles, mountains and trees on the pane, with no help from anyone! If she could only paint a picture that beautiful! Sophie bowed her head and said a little prayer.

"Dear Heavenly Father, I pray that I can paint beautiful pictures some day, but for now, just let me get my doll, in Jesus' name, amen."

Finally, finally, through the frosty pane Sophie saw Papa pulling up in front of the house, and heard Sarai scream, "They've come, the packages, they've come!"

Sophie walked slowly down the stairs. What if she didn't get her doll? What if she got a game or a book and she'd have to act happy and say politely, "Oh, it's just what I wanted!" Paper and boxes were scattered all over the dining room floor. Sarai and Bert raced around waving their gifts and Robby was pulling a little red wagon through the room with his sock doll in it. Mama handed Sophie a box and stood there waiting. The box was the right size, all right. Her hands were trembling as she tried to get it open. At last she got the cover off—and there she lay. The most beautiful doll in the world!

7

It seemed to Sophie as if the winter just flew by. The children often joined the Johnson kids on Saturdays to go sliding down the snowy hills in their pasture. Sometimes they would tie their sleds to the back of Papa's or Mr. Johnson's big sled and go skidding and swerving along behind until everyone had had a turn falling off into a snowbank. Sometimes they would choose sides, build snow forts and attack each other with snowball ammunition. Always, there was a bigger and better snowman in the process of construction. Papa was forever grabbing his old cap off a smiling snowman, or shouting, "Where's my new corncob pipe?" only to find it sticking out of the stomach of Robby's "butful" snowman!

When they were tired and covered all over with wet snow, the children would go rushing into the lean-to, where they stomped off the snow and took off their wet coats, caps and overshoes, then on into the warm kitchen for big mugs of cocoa and thick slices of Mama's fragrant, fresh bread.

"Bath time," called Mama. "Who's first?"

The big tin wash tub was standing in front of the glowing kitchen stove, full of steaming water. On a chair beside it was a large bar of Mama's 'Made at Home' soap.

"And," Mama added, "please be careful."

Sophie and Bert started to laugh and pointed at Sarai, who glowered at them. A week ago she had turned her bare bottom toward the open oven door. She'd had a hard time sitting down since. After their baths they climbed into their warm, flannel nightclothes and sat around the big heat-register, playing carrom until it was time to go racing upstairs to dive under the thick patchwork quilts. Before they knew it morning had arrived and Papa was calling, "Time to get up. Chores to be done."

Soon spring was showing signs of its approach. In a spell of warm weather, crocuses peeked out of the snow on the hillsides where the sun had beat the snowdrifts down. In every little valley there was a pond formed from the streams of melted snow-water rippling down from the hills. Then it turned cold again, and the ponds froze over. What fun it was, on their way to school, to race across the ponds on the 'rubber ice,' as they called it, and arrive breathless and triumphant on the other side. The oldest Johnson boy always went first, then yelled, "Next." Sophie always waited until last because she was really afraid of the 'rubber ice' that moved and groaned beneath one's feet. If she didn't go across they would all tease her and call her "sissy."

"Come on," yelled Bert, "last one across is a rotten egg!"

Sophie hesitated, took a deep breath and ran. She felt the ice shifting and the next thing she knew, she was in the icy cold water. She tried to crawl back onto the ice, but it kept breaking. The other children stood at the edge of the pond shouting advice and crying, except for Bert. He came running with a long, stout branch, crawled out on the ice as far as he could, thrust the branch out to Sophie and managed to pull her to shore. She never really remembered how Ed Johnson half-dragged, half-carried her back home. All she remembered was Mama's white face, and Papa and Mama getting her frozen clothes off, wrapping her in a big, warm quilt and putting her in their bed with a hot salt bag at her feet.

The next few weeks were like a dream. The doctor couldn't get out to the farm, as it had started to snow again, fiercely. Her ear hurt so very much. She kept pushing the quilt off because she was so hot. When she opened her eyes, the kerosene lamp that sat on the old secretary-desk seemed to be spinning around and around.

Finally one morning she woke up, opened her eyes and saw the kerosene lamp sitting solidly right where it belonged. She called out, "Mama, could I have my dolly?"

Mama came hurrying in, her face all smiles, carrying Dolly.

"Does your ear still hurt, Sophie?"

Sophie thought for a moment, then said, "Not awfully much, and I'm hungry. Could I have some milk toast?"

* * *

When spring truly came, it seemed that all in one day the ponds dried up, and the crocuses and cowslips that had peeked timidly out of the snow now covered the hillsides. Sophie stopped on the way to school to pick a bouquet for Miss Grimm. She always hurried around the place, now just a small damp spot, where the pond with the 'rubber ice' had been. *If it takes running across a pond with rubber ice to make me brave, I'll just be a coward—or a rotten egg!* she thought. *Anyway, now we'll be able to play run, sheep, run and ante-I-over again. Some of the bigger kids are playing baseball, but I don't think that would be much fun. I'm so glad that spring is here.*

* * *

"Is my sister dead?" Sophie heard a voice saying.

The voice seemed to come from a long distance away. She tried to see who was speaking but everything was black, and when she tried to turn her head, she seemed to spin around and around like the kerosene lamp through the darkness. There seemed to be a tall, dim figure moving toward her and she felt herself being lifted and carried, then laid down again. This hard place didn't feel like her bed.

"Put a coat over her," someone said. The voice seemed so loud and boomed in her ears. Someone was crying, "I didn't mean to, really I didn't."

"I want my own quilt that Mama made, over me," Sophie tried to say, but she didn't seem to be able to get the words out. She wanted to ask, "Whose sister is dead?"

She tried to raise her arm but it didn't seem to be there. That was odd. More talking echoed in her ears.

"Her Pa is coming. We found him out in his potato patch."

Papa would bring her quilt. She needn't worry.

Sophie felt a soft hand stroking her forehead and she smelled Mama's soap. The bed wasn't hard anymore, and her quilt was tucked around her. She would just go to sleep and not think about a dead sister.

Something touched her head. She tried to focus her eyes on who was there, and saw a blurry Robby. He was patting her face when he saw her trying to look at him, he ran out yelling, "My sister not dead!"

Mama and Papa ran in, then Sarai and Bert, crowding around the bed. A strange man spoke from the other side of the bed, "I am Dr. Schmidt. How do you feel?"

Sophie lifted her head a little and tried to raise the arm that hadn't been there. It was very weak, but she could feel it now. Then she remembered—

"Whose sister is dead?"

Everyone began talking at once.

"We thought you were!"

"We love you. . . ."

"We were so scared. . . ."

"Can you talk?"

Then Sophie seemed to remember, as if from very long go, playing tag in the school playground and running—when something hit her forehead, she felt a shattering pain—dazzling fireworks exploded before her eyes—and then darkness! Later it seemed as if there voices all around her . . . she was being carried . . . was in her own bed at home. Now she just wanted to sleep and let the room, the doctor, Mama, Papa, Sarai, Bert and Robby just fade away.

Sophie awoke the next morning feeling dizzy and weak. Her head ached and there was a bandage over her left eye. When she reached up to touch it, she felt a sharp pain shoot through her head. Robby came in, trying to tiptoe but falling over his own feet. He had Dolly dangling by the feet in one hand and his sock doll in the other. His face was covered with butter, jelly, and a big grin.

"I love you and Dolly loves you too," he said as he deposited both dolls on the bed. He patted Sophie's cheek, and she reached up to take his sticky, grubby little hand in hers. She didn't even know when he pulled back his hand, planted a wet, smeary kiss on her face and went trudging out of the room.

A little later Amy Johnson came in, her eyes red if she had been crying. She stood on one foot, then the other, and finally said, "I didn't mean to hit you with the baseball bat, honestly I didn't. I didn't know you were behind me."

She took her hands from behind her back and handed Sophie a doll dress.

"I made it all by myself. I hope it fits Dolly." Sophie took the dress and laid it on Dolly.

"Oh, it's a perfect fit." She took Amy's hand and squeezed it, saying, "You are my very best friend," then hugged Dolly to her and closed her eyes as Amy tiptoed out.

8

Sarai came running upstairs with her new blue polka-dotted dress over her arm. She had grown a lot this past summer and would need all new clothes to take to high school. Mama had received a huge box of beautiful clothes from Aunt Susan, who lived in Iowa and was wealthy. All of the clothes were made of beautiful material, but all were too big for Mama or Sarai. Both girls had been busy for days ripping out seams and pressing fabric flat, as Mama, her feet flying on the pedals of her old Singer sewing machine, made Sarai an entire new wardrobe out of the fine material. With a sigh, Sarai asked, "Mama, couldn't you make one of my dresses just a little smaller? I promise to try to lose a little weight. And, Mama, can you let it be . . . well, kind of citified?"

Mama looked at her steadily until Sarai dropped her gaze. Then Mama took her oldest daughter's hands in hers and said, "Dear girl, we are farmers and proud to be farmers. Besides, you are still a young girl. A pretty one, I'd say, but there will be plenty of time in your life to wear fancy clothes. You are going to high school to study and grow, in your mind and your body. When you are truly grown up, you will know what is really important in life. Now, hold still while I try this on you. A nice white collar and cuffs will really show off your beautiful complexion."

Sarai reddened a bit but smiled at Mama. To Sophie she said, "Just think, Sophie, I'm actually going to leave home and go to high school, in just one month. I can't believe it! I'm getting kinda scared. Maybe I won't be able to find my way to school and maybe I won't know how to act with so many kids in such a big school. What if they don't like me? Will my new clothes look funny? At least my blue dress is 'store-bought.' Oh, dear, do I have to go?"—and she was nearly in tears.

In the city she would stay with two old ladies, Miss Williams and Miss Rogers. The widowed Miss Williams kept house for her sister, and Miss Rogers, who had never married, was a first grade teacher. Papa would bring Sarai home for weekends until they got snowed in at the farm. Sophie thought, *I'll miss her so much. I'll have no one to keep me warm in bed, no one to whisper and giggle with when we're supposed to be asleep. But next year I'll be going to high school and I can stay with Sarai in the same place. Someone is always telling me that I will be too young to go away to high school, but anyway, by then Sarai will know how to act in a big school and she'll help me. She says that there are at least thirty boys and girls in the freshman class alone. That's too scary to even think of.*

*   *   *

It was a Thursday night, and Sophie was busy packing her best flannel nightgown, toothbrush, clean underwear and comb in a drawstring bag that Mama had made for her out of a flour sack. She was glad that the new hundred-pound flour sacks were pretty, with flowers on them, instead of the old ones that were plain white and had letters on them saying what kind of flour and how many pounds it weighed. Mama used to bleach the letters out and make bloomers from the sacks to wear for every day. Some of the children's mothers didn't bleach them, and sent their children to school wearing bloomers saying "Flour, 100 Lbs," or something like that. If the girls' dresses blew up the other kids would tease them. Sophie thought, *Mama would never do that.* She could hardly wait for tomorrow to come. One of her best friends, Amelia, had invited her to go home with her Friday night after school and stay until Papa picked her up Saturday afternoon. Never before had she spent a night away from home except on Christmas Eve at Grandpa and Grandma's.

Sophie felt so grownup. "Just think. Me, Sophie, going all by myself without Sarai, Bert or Robby along." Now there'd be something to tell Sarai when she came home for the weekend. Sarai always had those wonderful stories to tell about 'Life in the Big City': she had made a new friend to walk to school with; the boy who sat ahead of her in English class had passed her a note saying that he thought she was cute; and her algebra teacher had praised her in front of the whole class! High school must be so exciting! ". . . and what do I have to tell her about? That Bert wipes the dishes now since she's gone and that Sunday Biscuit had twin calves?" Sophie crawled into bed and wished Sarai were there so she could cuddle up to her warm back.

Friday morning, Sophie woke up and jumped out of bed and into her clothing before Papa even had to call her. Today was the first day of her big adventure. She gulped her breakfast down, brushed her teeth, threw on her coat and stocking cap and tugged on her overshoes and mittens. When Papa drew up in front of the house with the sled, she was jumping from one foot to the other, impatient to hop in. Mama came out the door carrying her lunch pail and drawstring bag. Hugging Sophie tight, she said, "Now, remember your manners and don't talk with food in your mouth. And be sure you go to the toilet before you go to bed! Now be a good girl."

"I will, I will. Goodbye, Mama, goodbye, Robby," called Sophie.

When they reached the gate by the calf pasture, she turned to look back. Mama was holding Robby, and they were still waving. The last thing she saw was Robby throwing her a kiss.

Amelia met her at the schoolhouse door with a big smile, and hand in hand they went into the schoolhouse.

Finally, four o'clock came. Amelia and Sophie rushed to get into their coats and were the first ones to scamper out the door. There was Amelia's father, sitting in an old-fashioned sleigh with high curved runners that reminded Sophie of pictures of Santa's sleigh. He was bundled up, a fur cap pulled down on his head, his thick eyebrows beaded with frost and a smile like Amelia's on his face. As the girls hopped up into the back of the sleigh, he said, "So you are Amelia's good friend Sophie. It is cold. You must stay under the feather quilt, where you will be warm. We will be home, soon."

Sophie remembered what Mama had told her about manners.

"Thank you, thank you very much."

It seemed only minutes before they pulled up in front of a large white house. Behind it Sophie could see a huge hip-roofed barn, a granary, a chicken house and a pig-sty. They were all painted red, and glistened with the snow on the roofs and icicles hanging from the eaves. A windmill whirled busily by a round wooden tank, where black and white cattle jostled each other to get a drink. There was even a rooster weathervane on the roof of the barn. She thought the whole farm looked like a picture from *The Dakota Farmer* magazine that came to Mama in the mail.

When the girls went into the warm, bright kitchen and Sophie saw Amelia's mother standing by the stove, she felt right at home. Amelia's mother beamed at her, came right up and took her in her arms.

"You are my girl's best friend, so you are my little friend also. Are you hungry? I have fresh Kase Kuchen. Sit here."

Sophie found herself sitting at a long table covered in a bright red-checkered oilcloth, with a glass of milk and a huge piece of coffee cake in front of her. It was sooo good!

When they finished eating, the girls went into the parlor. It was cool, and so orderly that Sophie felt as if she should stand very straight and salute the rows of stiff chairs that stood against the wall. They had starched, white crocheted doilies over their backs that looked like collars on a row of very dignified gentlemen. There was a fern standing at attention on a mahogany plant stand, and an old organ topped with a lace doily on which a Bible rested. Sophie was so busy surveying everything that she didn't notice her friend placing her drawstring bag down by a beautiful, ornately-carved wardrobe at the end of the room. Then Amelia said, "We get to sleep in here tonight. It will be so much fun. I usually sleep with my sister upstairs."

Sophie stood still. Were they to sleep on the floor? But Mama had told her it was impolite to ask too many questions, so she just said, "Thanks, Amelia. I'm so glad I could come. Your mama and papa are so nice and your mama's coffee cake is so good."

Amelia took her out to see the new kittens and her pet calf. The mother cow had refused to accept the new calf, so Amelia got to raise it. Sophie was allowed to feed the little calf the warm milk from a bottle. Oh, what fun it was to be here!

Supper was a little scary. Amelia's father waited at the head of the table until all of the children were standing behind their chairs. Then he said, "Now we pray."

The next thing Sophie knew everyone was down on their knees except the two girls. Amelia pulled frantically on Sophie's sleeve and she landed with thump on her knees. Mr. Wohl began to pray—and pray and pray! All at once Sophie's stomach growled loudly. Amelia's father hesitated for a moment, then went on with his prayer. Sophie's stomach gave another loud rumble, and she felt Amelia's whole body shaking as she tried to stifle a giggle.

"Amen," said Mr. Wohl.

Everyone got up and sat in their chairs and began to eat. It was quiet, with no sound but the clicking of silverware against dishes, when suddenly Amelia's big brother broke out in a roar of laughter. Soon everyone else joined in, including Mr. Wohl. At last he stopped laughing, wiped tears from his eyes and looked around the table.

"How happy we are to have our little friend Sophie here. But I think we all need to go to bed soon. Morning comes early; the cows don't wait."

Amelia and Sophie did the dishes, then went into the cold parlor. Sophie found out where they were going to sleep when Amelia opened up the wardrobe doors. Lo and behold, there was a bed, standing on end, waiting to be lowered to the floor. With the bed came a fat feather tick to lie upon, a feather quilt to put over them and big, fluffy down pillows. What fun it was to whisper and giggle under that wonderful, cozy quilt until they went to sleep. Very early the next morning, Sophie heard someone coming quietly into the room. She peeked with one eye and saw Amelia's mother standing by the bed. She felt the feather quilt being lifted, very carefully, and something being placed right below their feet. What could it be? She waited until all was still, then moved down and pushed the object with her foot. It was a large, round covered pan, wrapped in what seemed to be a towel. Sophie pulled her feet up, rolled herself into a round ball as far away from the mysterious object as possible, and tried to go to sleep again, but thoughts went whirling around and around in her head. It couldn't be anything dangerous. They were such nice people. Was it something meant to punish her, because her stomach had been so unruly last night? But she couldn't help that—and anyway, everyone had laughed and been so nice to her afterwards. Or might it be because she hadn't known about getting down on your knees when praying. She would ask Papa and Mama if their family could do that, from now on.

Sophie was glad when she felt Amelia stirring.

"Amelia," she whispered, "your mother put something under the covers, down by our feet. It feels warm. Was she afraid we were cold?"

Amelia laughed and whispered back.

"No, it is to keep the bread dough warm so it will rise, and she can make more of those Kase Kuchens that you liked so well. The house is cold until the fires in the stoves start burning well. We are keeping the bread dough warm. It is not keeping us warm!"

There was fresh, warm bread and Kuchen for breakfast and delicious sausage. Mr. Wohl watched Sophie as she ate, then said, "I see you like our food. You come, again, sometime. And you can watch us make our good sausage."

He turned to Mother Wohl.

"We must send some sausage home with our new little friend."

It was Saturday and Papa came driving up in the big old sled—too early, Amelia and Sophie thought, but they hugged and told each other that they would see each other on Monday, and that they would always be best friends. Sophie thanked Amelia's mother and father, then climbed in with Papa and away they went for home. She was quiet, thinking of all the things she would be able to tell about. The wonderful Kase Kuchen, the sausage that she was bringing home for her family to taste, the pet calf she got to feed and the wardrobe bed, the feather quilt and the bread dough that she had helped to make rise with her warm feet. Finally, Papa said, "Well, Sophie girl, did you have a good time?"

Sophie cuddled up to Papa, smiled up at him and answered, "Papa, it was so much fun. It was almost like being in a different country. I loved their feather quilts and their sausage, their coffee cake, and praying on our knees. We need to pray on our knees."

Papa thought for a while.

"Your mother and I will talk about that. The Wohls are good people."

Sophie was bursting with all she had to tell that night at the supper table. The one thing she didn't mention was how her stomach had betrayed her right in the middle of the prayer.

9

School would soon be over for the summer. Sophie had learned to slide swiftly over ice without falling in (when there was ice), but she never did learn to play baseball, or ever again go near where the older kids were playing. Amelia and Sophie used to walk behind the school barn to pick wild flowers and talk about the coming year when Sophie would be going away to high school. Amelia didn't know whether she would get to go to high school. Her parents believed that children should stay home and help on the farm; they should marry someone from a nearby farm, then buy their own farm in the same neighborhood. Both of the girls felt sad, thinking they might never be able to spend much time together after this year. They promised each other that they would always stay best friends, no matter what. Sophie thought that she would probably marry someone whom she met in college, and live far away in a big city where she would be a writer or an artist, or even a famous dancer. Her husband would be very proud of her and would bring their children to watch her dance. She said, "Amelia, how many children do you think you might have?"

Amelia's face got red. She said, "I suppose I might have quite a few to help on our farm."

After talking, they always felt a little shy with each other. When the bell rang they ran for the schoolhouse, afraid they might be late. They handed their bouquets of flowers to the teacher. She thanked them and never scolded if they were a wee bit late.

* * *

The hot, dry summer seemed to Sophie to fly by in a blaze of activity. The time was almost here when she would join Sarai, going away to high school. She was only twelve, and would be two years younger than the other ones in her class. She still liked to play with her doll, and Sarai warned her, "Don't try to take Dolly to high school. It would embarrass me to death if any of my friends found out about it."

She looked at Sophie with her 'high and mighty' look and said, "Just remember, Sophie, you will have to make some friends of your own. You can't always be with me. You are such a baby. You and my friends would never understand each other." Sophie said nothing, but she thought, *I'd better take Dolly. If Sarai doesn't want me with her, and if I don't make any friends, at least I'll have Dolly for comfort.*

* * *

It was so hot that after Sophie hung out the wash, she sat near the clothesline letting the wet clothes blow toward her with her feet in a tub of cold water right from the well. How wonderful it would be if Mama took them over to the pond to cool off. The pond was a man-made pool about halfway between home and town, at a spot where the railroad ran over a small hill. The hill was clay, rather than the rich loam of the fields. Italian workers, who had come many years before to work on the railroad, had dug deep holes into the clay bank below the railroad tracks, for ovens to bake their bread. Mama said that they used to start a fire in a hole and when it burned out leaving glowing embers, they put in their loaves of bread, covered the hole tightly, and the bread came out golden brown. Sophie puzzled over this but Mama said to never mind, as that is what she had heard tell. The little shacks the Italians had lived in there were long gone, but the deep pool they had dug for bathing and swimming remained, and stayed full of fresh water well into summer. Papa said there might be an underground spring there, feeding it. If the children got their Saturday morning work done on time, they could throw their towels and extra clothing into the old Model T and have time to go get groceries and stop at the pool on the way home. First they would paddle in the warm water for a while. Then if they felt really daring, Bert would strip to his underpants, Sophie and Sarai to their bloomers and undershirts, and practice swimming. Robby, in his underpants, played in the water, dipping it into a syrup pail with one of Mama's old spoons, or he might lie down in the shallow water near the edge, moving his arms and legs and shouting, "I'm whimming, I'm whimming!"

There usually wasn't anyone else there and sometimes even Mama waded in up to her waist, then sat in the sun to dry herself while she crocheted or tatted. What fun it was!

"Mama," said Sophie, as she watched her put down another basket of wet clothes to be hung on the line to dry, "when are we going to the pond? We haven't been there all summer."

"I know. But it's been a busy summer, what with music lessons for you girls, getting Sarai's and your clothes sewn for school, and then there was the time that you two—" Mama stopped and looked sternly at Sophie, "—let the cattle stray again when you went looking for that old vacant house that you weren't supposed to be looking for. Yes, it's been a busy summer. And that reminds me; this afternoon is your piano lesson."

Sarai and Sophie were taking lessons from Miss Pickens, a retired school teacher who lived on a farm about six miles away. Sophie frowned.

"But, Mama, I want to be a dancer, a writer or even a famous artist. I don't want to play the piano."

"Sophie."

That was all that Mama said. Ashamed, Sophie got up and started to hang out the wash.

But one o'clock in the afternoon the two of them were bumping along on the rough, graveled road on their way to Miss Picken's farm. Mama looked flushed and tired, her hair loose from her bun and hanging over her face. She yawned loudly. All at once the car started weaving over the loose gravel, went off the road, landed in the ditch, and stalled with a noise like a tired old horse who had just taken its final breath. Sophie had been staring at the gyrating road and clutching the side of the door frame when she heard Mama let out what sounded like a cross between a scream and a yawn. She let go of the door and turned to look at Mama. Her mouth was wide open, and she was still making those horrible noises as she tried to pull something out of her mouth.

"Mama!" Sophie cried. Something came out in her mother's hand. There sat Mama with her head back and her eyes closed, holding her bottom dentures. She began to cry and to laugh at the same time.

"Mama, what happened?"

She turned toward Sophie, wiping her tears and sliding the dental plate back in her mouth.

"I yawned and my teeth, the fake ones that is, turned sideways and I almost choked to death. I thought I'd never get my mouth closed. . . . Oh my, look what happened to our car! Papa will have a fit."

She started to cry again, then to laugh and pretty soon Sophie joined her. It was hard to tell whether the tears that were rolling down their cheeks were from laughing or crying. There was Papa's treasured old Model T in the ditch and no way that they could get it out.

"Mama, why don't you push and I'll pull?"

They began to laugh again until their stomachs ached.

"Well," Mama said, "we will have to walk home and get Papa to pull it out with his team of horses. And Sophie—we don't mention teeth. Remember. The car hit some loose gravel. Papa needs to talk to the Township Board about keeping up these roads."

"Mama, Papa is ON the Township Board. Okay, I won't mention teeth. But what if Papa asks me what happened?"

Mama looked sternly at Sophie for a moment.

"We DID hit gravel . . . and by the way, when do you want to go to the pool?"

Papa pulled the old flivver out of the ditch without asking too many questions.

"Well, the board needs to do something about that road. I'll bring it up at the next town meeting."

Mama found time to take them to the pool several times that summer.

* * *

"Sophie, get up."

Mama's voice sounded a little cross. Sophie crawled out of the warm cocoon she had made for herself after Sarai got up. She remembered, vaguely, hearing Sarai say, "I'm going to get up now even if you aren't. I'm going to bring in some water from the rain barrel and shampoo my hair with some of that new stuff Mama bought from the Watkins man, before Mama decides to put it up in her special cupboard space."

Sophie remembered thinking, *She's getting really fussy about her hair. She doesn't want to use plain old hand soap on it anymore. Is that what happens when you begin to grow up and go away to high school? Is that what will happen to me?* Then Sophie rolled back into her cocoon and went soundly back to sleep, to dream that her hair had grown down to her feet, and that when she let it down into the rain barrel to shampoo it, something grabbed it and started to pull her in.... She was saved by Mama's voice. This time it sounded as if she had better get right up or there would be real trouble.

Quickly she dressed and slid down the banister. Mama was rushing around the kitchen "like a house afire" as Papa often said. She looked upset, muttering to herself, "I'll never be ready for tonight."

Of course. Sophie remembered: tonight was Mama's turn to entertain the Whist club. It was her last chance to have a party before the threshing season started—and while she had both girls to help before school started. Sophie thought, *Am I actually going away to high school? I don't think I really want to go.*

"Sophie, I want you to dust the furniture in the parlor and in the dining room. Sarai, get the good dessert plates out of the china closet and wash them. Oh, and there's the silverware to polish."

Mama put a big iron kettle of lard on the stove to melt.

"Sophie, I need some fresh eggs from the chicken

coup. I heard a lot of cackling out there a few minutes ago, so there should be some fresh ones."

Sophie dropped the dust-cloth and ran out the door to the hen house. "Broody," her pet hen, had just laid a big brown egg and was announcing it loudly.

"Broody, who will take care of you when I'm away to school?"

She gathered the warm, brown eggs in her apron and walked carefully back to the house, then returned to the dusting. In the kitchen Mama could be heard furiously beating eggs, and Sophie could smell the rosettes sputtering in the hot lard. Mama would serve rosettes topped with raspberries and whipped cream to her guests that night. Papa would take his pipe out of his mouth and say, smiling proudly, "Yessir, my wife is the best darned cook in Kidder County."

But Sophie said to herself, "How I do love Mama's rosettes with lots of raspberries and whipped cream on them, and those darned Whist players will eat them all."

Supper was a quick affair. As soon as everyone was through eating, Mama went into the bedroom to get dressed, the girls washed the dishes and saw that the parlor and dining room were 'spick and span,' while Papa and Bert did the milking, cream-separating, and fed the calves as well as the numerous cats that hovered near. Robby kept saying, "I help too," until Sophie gave him a towel and a pan to wipe and put away. When Mama came out of the bedroom the entire family stared. Sophie tossed the towel on the back of a chair and ran to throw her arms around her mother. Mama smelled so delicious and looked so beautiful. Her hair was marcelled, her cheeks were rosy, her eyes twinkled and even the long apron that covered the dress she had made, the apron that would be whipped off as soon as the guests started to arrive, didn't stop her from looking like a queen!

How Sophie wished that they could stay downstairs just this one time. All too soon Mama called, "Time to go to bed, children. Bert, you may read to Robby."

Feet dragging, they began to mount the stairs. Bert called back, "But it's too early to go to bed."

Papa's voice came booming up the stairway: "Did you hear what your Mother said?"

In no time they were all in their bed-clothes and tucked in. Sophie lay there with her eyes closed, half asleep. She heard the company arrive, all the cars wheezing and coughing as they came to a standstill in front of the house. Soon the house was filled with laughter and talk and the sound of chairs scraping the floor, as the company settled around the dining room table for that all-important game of Whist.

"Sophie, get up. Hurry."

It was Bert's voice, speaking in a whisper, close to her ear. Sophie opened her eyes. There stood Sarai, Bert and Robby, their eyes sparkling in the moonlight that poured into the room.

"We're going to listen at the register. Maybe we can learn how to play Whist." Though Sarai looked a bit reluctant and drawled, "How childish," soon all four were sprawled on their stomachs on the floor around the register that brought the heat up from the dining room. Their eyes and ears were taking turns trying to see and hear what that mysterious Whist game was all about.

"Why do grownups have all the fun?" whispered Bert.

All at once there was complete silence. Then everyone seemed to be talking at once. Suddenly Mr. Olson's voice roared out, "I shot for the moon and I made it!"

What did that mean? They were supposed to be playing Whist. The children looked at each other, then got to their feet and tiptoed to the window. Even Sarai was pushing and shoving to get a good look at the moon. It was there, round, orange and undamaged. They could see no bullet holes of any kind in it.

Robby began to whimper and Bert took him back to bed. Sarai and Sophie pulled their thick quilt around them and lay quietly, each with her own thoughts. Then Sarai whispered, "They could have let me, at least, stay downstairs. I'm older. I have even been away to high school."

She turned over with her back to Sophie. Soon the company left, after many happy goodbyes shouted back and forth, and the house became quiet. Soft footsteps sounded on the stairs. Sophie raised her head from her pillow and listened. Who could it be? Then she heard a soft, sweet voice say, "You had better eat fast so that you don't get too cold."

The moonlight shining on Mama's smiling face made her look like a mischievous angel with a halo, as she came into the room carrying a tray of rosettes topped with strawberries and whipped cream. After the girls ate their treats, Sarai turned over again and went to sleep.

Sophie lay thinking about grownups. "They do funny things, loving things, grumpy things. Will I be like that when I grow up? Will I be more funny, more loving or more grumpy? Do I really want to grow up? I guess I do. Just so I can find out what I will be like." Sophie patted her full stomach, thought about how loving and funny Mama was, and well, a little grumpy sometimes too, and then wondered, "What does 'Shoot for the moon and make it' mean?" Perhaps that was a grownup secret.

*   *   *

Saturday was cleaning day. It was Sophie's job to dust the parlor. As soon as it was done, she cranked up the old phonograph to play "Second Hand Rose" sung by Fanny Brice, while she danced from one piece of furniture to the other, admiring the shine that lemon oil had given each piece. Dusting was fun; she loved to look at old family pictures as she carefully lifted them to dust underneath, then polished the glass and set them back in their places until next Saturday when she came to dust them again. The people in the photos all looked so grim. No one smiled. *I wonder why,* she thought. Was it because of the stiff, high collars that the men wore? Or because of the way the women had their hair scraped back from their faces? Maybe they all had bad teeth.

It was fun to spin the big, revolving bookcase around and look at all of the wonderful books that she hadn't read. How she loved to read, but Mama said that most of these books were a little "old" for her, whatever that meant. What a lot of books, just waiting for her to get older. She had gone through many of them while she was getting well after being hit by a baseball bat. She could read most of the words but couldn't understand what they meant. Mama's instruction books that she had used when teaching school, were there too. "Well," Sophie said, out loud to herself, "maybe I'll wind up being a teacher like Mama. Right now, dusting is my favorite job."

When Sophie walked into the dining room, dust cloth in hand, Mama was just walking out, carrying the mop and mop pail. She turned and saw Sophie.

"Dear, the floor is still wet. Sit down in Papa's chair for a bit, until it dries." How Sophie loved to sit there, to take off her shoes and rest her feet on the clean braided rug that lay in front of Papa's chair. The sun streamed through the dining room window, touching Mama's red geranium on the windowsill and the white curtains that framed the window, with gold; making a bright path across the rug. There were still wet streaks on the newly mopped linoleum. What a beautiful picture it all made. "I could paint it," Sophie said to herself. Then she began to sing softly, "I'm happy, happy, happy." Mama stuck her head in the doorway and asked, "What is it, honey girl?"

"I'm just singing because I'm so happy, because I love rag rugs and fluffy white curtains and red geraniums and clean floors and sunshine and I especially love you." Mama set down the pail and mop with a thump. She came into the dining room, took Sophie into her arms dust cloth and all, and sang softly into her ear, "And I love, love, love you, too."

* * *

Sophie moved around as if in a dream. Was it really true? Could she really be going away to high school in just a few days? She was packing her new clothes in the big old leather suitcase from the attic, and wondering, "What will it be like to sleep in a strange bed at night? To be away from this cozy room? To not be awakened by the sun streaming through the east window? Will Robby and Goph miss me?" With a little shake of her head she turned to the sturdy box she had found to hold her good shoes, overshoes and heavy coat. That was done, and she had just finished packing the suitcase when Mama came in, looked around and said, "It looks as if you are all ready to go."

Sophie was frantically trying to get the suitcase closed and fastened before Mama noticed the strange bulge in it.

"Let me help. Perhaps I can get the things arranged a little better."

She lifted the lid, started to smooth Sophie's best dress, then lifted it out, and there was Dolly!

"Sophie, you can't take Dolly to high school! Whatever are you thinking?"

"But, Mama, I'm only twelve years old and I love her and I'm not used to sleeping without her. Please, Mama, I'll work hard at school and have her to come home to at night. I'm not even a teenager yet. Oh, please!"

Mama thought for a moment.

"Well, dear, you take your Dolly. I guess you have to grow up in your own way." She smiled, gave Sophie a hug and left the room.

* * *

Sarai and Sophie sat on the bed in their tiny bedroom in 'Aunt Jennie's' house, looking at each other. Finally, Sarai said, "Now we're supposed to wash our hands and be at the table by six o'clock, or Miss will get a little frown on her face and say, 'When I was a young girl, we were taught to always be on time.' Sophie didn't want to go into the cramped, crowded dining room and sit down at the table with those two severe-looking old ladies. Sarai hadn't told her before that she should behave any differently than she did at home. Hadn't Papa and Mama taught her to be polite? Besides, she just wanted to sit for awhile and think about everything that had happened since early that morning, when Papa's voice boomed up the stairway.

"Girls, get out of bed. I need to get you up there and get back in time to start mowing hay."

He had sounded as if this were just an ordinary day.

Then followed the long, rough ride in the Model T, sitting in the back surrounded by all of their school things, with the side curtains flapping in the wind. Sophie held her heavy suitcase on her lap, although Papa had wanted to put it on the running board with Sarai's suitcase. What if he had noticed the bulging top, or what if it had fallen off and popped open? Dolly could have been run over or broken just from the fall! Still to face was Sarai's reaction when she found out that Dolly had come along. Would she tell the girls in school so they would laugh at Sophie?

At last they arrived. It had seemed so strange to walk into that little bungalow and be greeted by those two little old ladies. They seemed so old compared to Mama, even Grandma, and not at all cheerful like either one. The house seemed dark and smelled old, too. Sarai had helped her put away her things, but she managed to slip Dolly under her side of the bed wrapped in a petticoat when Sarai wasn't looking. Tomorrow she would have to walk with Sarai to that big, brick school house and meet the stares of all those strange boys and girls. Would they think her weird, a strange country hick? At least school work was not a worry; she loved learning and had always done all her lessons perfectly. But she would need friends too. How she wished that Amelia was going to be there. What would it be like to have more than one teacher and have to walk from one room to another for classes? Would she remember what room to go to? "Papa, Mama, please come and get me," she cried in her heart.

"Sophie, come on. We'll be in trouble."

Sophie began to cry.

"I don't want to be here. I want to go home. I miss Mama and Papa and Bert and Robby and Goph and Sunday Biscuit. I think I'm going to throw up."

Sarai tried to make her face look stern, the way

Mama did sometimes, then said, "I'll see if I can bring you a pan."

Sophie laid down on the bed and sobbed. Then she felt a soft hand on her forehead, and a warm blanket being laid tenderly over her. She raised her head. It was Miss Williams, a sweet smile on her wrinkled face.

"There, there, little Sophie. You'll be all right. You just lie there a bit and I'll bring you some milk toast. You can call me Grandma Minnie."

Milk toast! Just like Mama!

When Sarai came back in the room, she saw the plate, the milk toast all eaten, and Sophie lying there sound asleep with Dolly in her arms.

10

"Bert, you need to get me a cream-can of water from the windmill. Sophie, you need to go along and keep the can from tipping off the wagon. Don't turn the windmill too far into the wind or it might wreck the sails. And be sure to put the can's cover on as soon as it gets full, or we'll have a can of mud. Will this wind ever stop blowing?"

Mama didn't look like her usual sweet smiling self. Her hair had come loose from the bun on the back of her neck and a strand was hanging down across her face stubbornly refusing to be brushed away by her hand. Her face was red, glistening with sweat, and as grim as Papa's had been ever since the wind started blowing day after day like a demon with the sole desire of wiping out the whole world. Sophie wanted to say, "Mama, can't we wait until a little later? Maybe it will quit blowing so hard." But when Bert looked at her sternly and started out the door, she knew she had better follow. The wind pushed past them relentlessly as they struggled up the hill, pulling the wagon with the can. The tank by the windmill was full of water but the cattle were huddled by the barn, not even wanting to come get a drink. At least no one would have to go out to the pasture after them tonight. Sunday Biscuit's bag wasn't dripping milk, as it usually did. There wouldn't be a full can of cream to take to town Saturday night, and therefore no ice cream cones or fun walking around town with the Johnson girls. On the way back to the house, the wagon seemed to have a mind of its own and kept nipping at Bert's heels. Sophie had a hard time keeping the can upright while she tried to help Bert slow the wagon down. At last they got to the house. Mama took one look at them, and for the first time all day, a smile spread across her face.

"Hurry and get washed. Go easy on that water—you two just found out how hard it is to get. Papa should be here any minute now. That is, if the old 'Tin Lizzie' didn't get blown off the road."

Not long afterwards the door opened and in came Papa, carrying the mail. He dropped it on the table and headed for the sink. After he finished washing up, he picked up his newspapers and went into the dining room, sat down in his chair and began to read. Not a word had been spoken. Sophie started to say "Mama," when Mama put her finger over her mouth and motioned for the two children to go upstairs. They walked slowly up to the girls' room where they could talk without being heard downstairs.

"What do you suppose Papa is upset about? I haven't done anything, have you, Bert?"

"Well," Bert said, "I did come home early from weeding the potatoes but it was hard to even walk between the rows without being blown over. Usually, though, Papa doesn't act like this when we've done something wrong. He usually talks things over with us. Anyway, I don't think we'll have much of a potato crop this year—maybe he's worried because it doesn't look as if we'll have much of anything at all. I know Mama is worried."

They heard the outside door open and the voices of Sarai and Robby. Robby came running upstairs, with a big grin on his dirty face, to tell Bert and Sophie how much fun the two of them had had down at the Johnsons.

They had gone so that Robby could play with Billie while Sarai could visit with Amy. Bert always leered and said, "I know what Sarai and Amy are 'visiting' about: Boys!"

Then Mama called up the stairway, "Papa wants you children down here. And right away."

Never had Mama's voice sounded so serious. The children looked at each other. What was happening? Papa and Mama were not their usual selves. They were almost afraid to go down there. Sarai had just reached the top of the stairs on her way up. Now she turned around, saying, "Well, I'm the oldest, I guess I'd better go first. Let's not start asking questions. Just let's be quiet until they tell us what is going on."

With that speech, she went solemnly back down the stairs, followed by Bert, who actually walked instead of sliding down the banister and shouting, "I win!" Sophie took Robby's hand and whispered to him, "Everything will be all right. Mama and Papa love us a lot and they'll fix anything that is wrong."

They marched into the dining room and sat down at their usual eating places. Papa's head was bowed. Mama reached over and stroked his hands that were crossed on the table. Everyone sat quietly, waiting for Papa to speak. Finally he lifted his head. His eyes looked red as if he had been crying.

"Children, something very sad has happened. Do you remember when your mother and I took all four of you children to the bank? It was a very important occasion, because we were going to open a savings account for each of you so that you would have money for college. Since then each of you have added money to your account by weeding potatoes, herding cattle up by the big hill, helping Mama take care of her vegetable garden, and in many other ways. Remember, when you first went to the bank a kind man came out and told you how wise you were to start a savings account for college. . . ."

Robby interrupted, "Papa, is my money still in that bank?"

Papa raised his hands to his forehead, bowed his head again, then looked at Robby.

"That is part of what I am about to tell you, Robby. As you children know, we have had very little rain for a time, and our crops have not yielded well. All over our wonderful country there have been problems. People have a hard time even getting enough to eat. Lots of farmers have had their farms taken away from them by the banks because they couldn't pay what they owed them. Now many of the banks are in trouble and are failing. I won't try to explain what that means, but the banks cannot handle money anymore. Children, the money that your mother and I and each of you had in the bank is no longer there."

They sat in stunned silence. How could a bank just lose someone's money? Robby raised his hand as if he were in school and said, "Papa, I'll just pull more weeds for Mama and make more money for all of us and put it in a new bank."

Papa almost smiled.

"Robby, you're a fine boy. I know that all four of you children will help in any way you can. What a fine family we have, Mama."

The room was very quiet. Papa seemed ready to tell them something further. He got out his big red handkerchief, blew his nose hard and wiped his eyes.

"Now I must tell you about a very sad thing that happened because of the bank failure. Do you remember Mr. Larken, the man who came and talked to you that day? He was the bank president. He felt so very bad because of the bank failing and because so many people lost their money—for we weren't the only ones that did—that he took his own life."

Mama looked at Papa as if to say, "Aren't the children a little young to hear about that?" But Papa went on.

"I wondered if I should tell you about that, but as you grow up you will find that many sad things happen and that you must learn how to handle them."

Sophie spoke up.

"Papa, could we pray for him the way Amelia's family does?"

In a few moments everyone was on their knees while Mama said a prayer for Mr. Larken and his family. Then she got up, wiped tears from her eyes and bustled to the kitchen. Soon everyone was drinking hot cocoa and eating Mama's warm bread. Not even Robby felt like talking, and soon they were all tucked in bed. Sophie lay quietly, unable to go to sleep for thinking about what had happened. She thought of how sad Mr. Larken's family must be feeling. Then she thought of the college money being all gone. Would she be able to earn enough money, somehow, to go to college? The murmur of Mama's and Papa's voices drifted up through the heat register, and all at once a warm feeling spread over her entire body as she cuddled down under her warm comforter. How lucky they were to have these parents. She knew that, no matter what happened, Papa and Mama would always be there for their children.

11

The old pump handle squeaked like the sound of unwilling chalk being dragged across a blackboard. The sound made Sophie cringe, but she had to hurry and get that pail of water into the house. *Why are grownups in such a hurry, always?* she thought. The pump stood under an ancient oak tree. Squirrels chattered as they ran up and down the trunk, dropping acorns on the grass as they climbed. Sophie loved this cool, dim place, especially at this time of the evening when it was just dark enough that she wasn't seen by people passing by but not dark enough to be scary. As she pumped, she thought about school and how fast the past two years had flown. She loved high school now, had many friends, and teachers admired the perfect papers she turned in.

When 'Aunt Jennie' died, and 'Grandma Minnie' retired from teaching first grade and moved to a niece's home in another town, Sophie felt bad. She had learned to love the two kind old ladies, the dark little cottage and the tiny bedroom she and Sarai had shared. Wistfully she remembered the vine that twined around the small window, of the robin which had made her nest in it, of the baby robins who chirped early in the morning and awakened her. Now she was working for her board and room at the home of Mr. and Mrs. Adolph. They were kind, but they just weren't Grandma Minnie and Aunt Jennie. Sarai worked for another family, and was interested only in boys and her own friends. As Sophie stood there pumping, she thought about Dolly. *Maybe,* she thought, *it's time for me to leave her back home on the farm. I'll put her in her grape-basket bed and if I get married and have a little girl, I'll give Dolly to her. I'll miss Dolly, but I'm a teenager now....*

"Hello."

A strange voice startled her. She grabbed the pail off the faucet, spilling water on her shoes in her haste to run to the house.

"Wait. I came to ask you something. I talked to your father and mother and they said it was all right. I want to take you to Richard Dempsey's boxing match in Bismarck next Friday night."

Sophie was speechless for a moment, then looked up just enough to recognize Ned Brockman standing in the shadows, his hat in his hand and his sturdy legs planted firmly in the damp grass. Ned lived on a farm not far away, but he had never paid any attention to her. He was always talking to Sarai.

"Papa and Mama said I could go? Then . . . then I will," Sophie stuttered.

"Okay, I'll pick you up Friday night about 5:00. It's quite a ways."

Sophie stepped into the faint light coming from the house and gave him a shy smile.

"Thank you very much."

He glanced at her and looked away. Then he looked back at Sophie with a shocked expression on his round face.

"Oh, wait—"

But Sophie was rushing toward the house, calling out, "I'll be ready and thank you so much. I've never been to a boxing match."

She burst in, slopping water on the floor in her hurry. Mrs. Adolph was sitting in the kitchen in her wheelchair. She frowned and said, "I told you to get a pail of fresh water in here and no lollygagging. Who were you talking to out there? I heard voices."

"A friend of our family's came over to ask me if I wanted to go to a boxing match in Bismarck. He said he had already asked Papa and Mama if it would be all right."

"You are only fourteen years old! It's a fright that your parents would let you go clear to Bismarck without your family. But you say you are going with a family friend? Well, who am I to say no. You had just better have your work all done before you even think of leaving."

The way she rolled her wheelchair into the parlor spoke of her disapproval, but Sophie was too excited to care. *Is this a date? Am I going on a date? I don't much like him. He is too old and his hair is beginning to disappear.* . . . Her thoughts ran on. *I thought he liked Sarai. But oh, my first date! And I'm only fourteen. But if Papa said it was all right it must be all right.*

Friday night finally came. Sophie hurried home from school and rushed around putting meatloaf and baked potatoes in the oven. She was about to take off her apron when Mrs. Adolph wheeled into the kitchen, fixed her eagle eyes on Sophie and said, "You aren't through yet, young lady. I want you to dust the parlor and take the sweeper to the carpet."

Sophie had to bite her lip to keep from saying, "But I always do that on Saturday." She quickly finished the parlor, then rushed to her room and put on her "Sunday-go-to-meeting" dress and her new slippers, combed her hair, then found the little tube of Tangee lipstick that she had spent her ice cream money for at Woolworth, and tried to make her lips look like Clara Bow's in the picture at the theater. *I'm going to miss that ice cream cone,* she thought. She always tried to go easy on using composition paper so as to have at least five cents left at the end of the month from the money Mama sent her, the price of one ice cream cone. "Oh, I wish I had some perfume...." At the same time Sophie bought the lipstick, Sarai bought some Evening in Paris perfume that she had saved up for. "If we still lived together, we could share. But Sarai told me I was too young to be buying lipstick. I wonder what she'll think now."

A rap sounded on the front door. With her heart pounding and her knees knocking together, she went to open it. There stood Ned, his hat in his hand.

"Hello, I'll be right out."

Sophie ran to tell Mrs. Adolph that she was leaving.

"Well, behave yourself and remember, you have work to do tomorrow, so don't come in so late that you can't get up in the morning."

As she turned the chair around and swept away, Sophie heard her mutter, "Those parents! Where is their good common sense?"

Ned stood waiting. Should she have introduced him to Mrs. Adolph? Oh dear! He escorted her to the car and opened the back door for her to get in. She sat down, adjusted her skirt properly, then heard a familiar voice from the front seat.

"Well, Sophie, this is a surprise."

It was Vivien Johnson, all dressed up, sitting up front beside her boyfriend who was driving. Sophie sat there stunned. Vivien was older than Sarai, and her boyfriend was even older than Ned!

When Ned got in the back seat next to her, Sophie tried to smile politely and talk to him, but her nose was icy cold as it always got when she was sick or scared, and she had to squeeze her hands together to keep them from shaking. There was something funny going on. It seemed as if the three of them had a little private joke that wasn't to be shared with Sophie.

The boxing match was awful. *They're mean to each other,* she thought. *And pretty soon we'll be going home and what will happen then?* Sarai had told her never to let a boy kiss her on the first date. If he just put an arm across your shoulders it was all right. But Ned wasn't a boy. He was an old man! *I wish I was home! I even wish I had Dolly to hug!*

Sarai also said that unless your date was rich and took you to a restaurant, you usually stopped on the way home for a hamburger. If you did, and he was really handsome and nice, you must be sure to say, "No onions on mine!"—just in case he wants to give you a quick little good-night kiss at your door.

Sophie had to fight to stay awake in the car. She needn't have worried because all Ned did was reach over and pat her hand, which made her feel like saying, "Arf, arf!" They did stop for hamburgers; and in no time, it seemed, they were home. Ned walked her to the door. Sophie said, "Good night, I had a good time. Thank you for taking me."

Ned looked at her if he wanted to say something but changed his mind. He started to walk away, then turned back and said, "Thank you for going with us, Sophie, and, uh, tell Sarai hello for me."

As Sophie opened the door to go in, she thought she heard the three of them laughing as they drove off.

On Monday morning Sophie couldn't wait to tell Sarai about her date. Usually they walked uptown together on Saturdays after their work was done, to meet friends at the drug store, and—if they had managed to save nickels from the money Mama sent them for school supplies each month—buy big, dripping ice cream cones. On Sundays, Sarai usually picked Sophie up for church. But Sarai had been sick over this weekend, so they hadn't seen each other.

They always met at the end of the block and walked to school together. Finally Sophie would have a chance to tell her sister all about the date, and ask her if God might punish her for telling a lie: she had said she had enjoyed herself and she really hadn't, very much.

"You will never guess what I did Friday night, Sarai. You will never believe this, but I had a date! Don't worry, I remembered everything you told me. And he didn't even try to put his arm around me or kiss me." Sophie giggled. "You know how I like onions on my hamburgers and I even gave those up just in case—of course, I don't really like him much, he's too old. I hope he doesn't ask me again." Sarai stopped and fixed Sophie with an unrelenting stare.

"Just what will Papa and Mama say about this? Who was he, anyway? And I have something to tell you too."

"Oh, Sarai, Papa and Mama do know. They told him it was all right. It was just our neighbor, Ned. I thought he liked you. I almost forgot—he told me to tell you hello from him."

Sarai's face turned chalky white, then beet red. Sophie thought she was going to throw a tantrum right on the sidewalk. She clenched her fists.

"Oh, oh, oh, how could he? I'll never speak to him ever again. I got a letter from Mama saying that he had asked them permission to take me to the boxing match, and he didn't show up. I hate him, hate him, hate him."

Sarai began to cry and rushed toward the high

school, leaving poor, shocked Sophie standing alone on the sidewalk.

The next morning Sarai wasn't there to meet her, nor the next, nor the next. On the fourth morning Sophie was walking to school with her head down, paying no attention to the loud, happy school kids who were passing by. She was thinking that perhaps her dear sister would never again be standing at the end of the block waiting for her; that they would never again share secrets, or walk uptown on Saturdays or cuddle to get warm in their old bed on the farm, or even just giggle together.

All at once she felt a warm hand in hers and heard Sarai's voice.

"Guess what, Sophie. Ned thought you were me the other night! It was so dim under that big tree. He did intend to take me to the boxing match. He even asked me to go steady."

Sophie felt as if a dark cloud had lifted from overhead. She really hadn't wanted to go, and it hadn't been much fun. Since it was all a mistake she wouldn't even have to think of it as a 'First Date.' She had wanted her first date to be a dream come true, and now she would still have that to look forward to and dream about.

Sarai and Sophie smiled at each other. With their hands linked they went dancing on, each to her own music, to school.

* * *

Sophie shook her hand and rubbed it to wake it up, then dropped her arm down by the side of her desk and swung the hand back and forth. She loved algebra and was getting straight A's on her report card, but she had been working for some time on this assignment and was tired. That hand always went to sleep when she used it for a long time, and had ever since she had been hit in the head with a baseball bat. Suddenly something was thrust into her hand. She looked down and saw a small piece of paper. When Mr. Brown turned to the board to illustrate a problem solution, Sophie glanced quickly at the note: "meet me at the drugstore after school—Hannah." She turned her head and saw Hannah looking at her, with that mischievous look that mean she had something just a little naughty planned. Quickly, before Mr. Brown turned back from the board, Sophie nodded "Yes."

What exciting plan did Hannah have this time? Sophie couldn't wait to find out. The afternoon seemed to crawl by. Finally the closing bell rang. Sophie grabbed her coat and books from her locker and hurried to the drugstore. If she got home even five minutes late, Mrs. Adolph would complain. Hannah was already there, as she had special permission to leave school early because she worked at the drugstore soda fountain. She was making an ice cream soda for a customer when Sophie came in, and glanced up.

"Just take that booth. I'll be right there," she said, as if Sophie were another customer.

Sophie sat down, thinking, *Oh hurry, Hannah, I can't be late.* The cash register drawer went "ding" and a moment later Hannah slipped into the opposite seat in the booth. She looked around to see if anyone else had come in, then said in a low voice, "I think I can get a pack of you-know-whats by next Friday, if you can get some matches and think of a place where we could go."

Sophie stared at Hannah, her mouth open. The two of them had talked about how it might be fun to see what smoking was like, but she hadn't thought they would ever really try it. She had hoped that it was just another one of Hannah's wild ideas and would fade into thin air.

"Hannah, I don't know. I need to go now or I'll be in trouble."

"Well, Sophie, we did agree! Why don't you get some matches and think of a good, private place where we could go. We have to decide what kind of cigarettes we want to get, too. What an adventure this will be!"

Hannah was her best friend, and they'd whispered about this when Sophie had stayed overnight at her house. But what if they got caught? Papa would be so angry and Mama would feel so bad. Maybe they'd get expelled and she would have to go to some other school. What if, what if . . .

The notes flew back and forth for the rest of the week. Finally the plan was perfected. It was too late to turn back. They decided on Kools cigarettes; Friday night would be the night. Sophie knew she could get some matches from the box on the shelf above the kitchen stove. Would that be really stealing? A shiver ran down her spine. She could ask Mrs. Adolph's permission to have dinner and spend the evening with Hannah's family, if she promised to work extra hard Saturday morning. Everything was settled—except where to go. Where could they carry out this daring escapade?

One afternoon in class Sophie felt Hannah's eyes drilling into her back, and turned around. With a big grin on her face, Hannah slipped her another note: "I know the perfect place. Behind the old newspaper building. No one ever goes there."

The dilapidated building still had an ancient printing press on the main floor, and was supposed to be haunted by a man who had committed suicide in one of its many empty rooms. Everyone walked a little faster when they passed it, and no one but hobos ever went inside. There were all kinds of stories about what went on in there. Would the two of them actually have the nerve to sneak behind it—and at night? Sophie cringed at the idea of hiding behind that scary old building to try something that she really didn't want to do. The memory came back of the time long ago when she, Sarai, and the Johnson girls sneaked behind the hotel in town, to see that couple doing what they probably shouldn't have been doing. She remembered the arc of the lit cigarette as it left the unknown person's hand and shot to the ground. That was the moment she had decided that she never wanted to smoke. *Why am I trying it now?* she thought. *But Hannah is my best friend. She wants to, and I can't let her go there alone. Should I ask Sarai about it? No . . . better not.*

Friday finally came. Sophie had Mrs. Adolph's permission to spend the evening with Hannah's family, with the admonition: "That Hannah is too pretty for her own good. You'd better stay away from her." Sophie walked slowly to the drugstore and sat in a booth, giving Hannah a quick wink and a discreet 'thumbs-up.' Hannah gathered her things, said goodbye to Mr. Jones the druggist, and they hurried out.

It began to snow lightly and the wind whistled around the corner of the old building. What was that noise? It sounded like stealthy shuffling footsteps. Was it the town marshal, or just a hobo seeking a dry place to sleep? Hannah peeked around the corner while Sophie shivered and got ready to bolt back to the streetlights glowing dimly through the swirling snow.

"No one there," whispered Hannah.

She pulled the package of Kools out of her pocket.

"Quick, the matches!"

The wind blew harder and it seemed they would

never get the darn things to light. Sophie's hands were freezing and trembled as she tried again and again. "Oh, I wish I were home and Mama was smiling at me and saying, 'Get up to the table. Beef stew to warm cold tummies!'" How often she had said, "I hope we have pie for dessert, not peach sauce again." How wonderful peach sauce would taste right now. Finally the cigarette lit and smoke began spiraling up through the falling snow. Hannah was already puffing. Sophie took a drag or two, then sucked in her breath. Her head began to spin and her stomach heaved. She was going to throw up! "Oh, please, no...." She looked at Hannah, who was leaning against the sagging door, her face white as the flakes drifting down around them. Sophie dropped to her knees in the wet slush. As her stomach betrayed her, she heard Hannah half laughing, half crying and saw her toss the package of Kools on the sidewalk, where it soon was covered by the forgiving snow.

The walk home was silent. By the time they arrived, Sophie felt that her feet could not take one more step. Hannah took her hand for moral support as they opened the kitchen door and walked in. Hannah's mother sniffed the air and looked at their white, woebegone faces.

"Well. Supper is ready, if you girls feel like eating."

After the blessing was said, there was silence. Sophie and Hannah picked at their food, each wishing that someone would say something, scold them, send them to bed, anything! Finally Hannah's father paused in his eating and let his stern gaze move from one face to the other.

"Well, girls, I don't think you need a lecture, and you're too old to spank. I think you two have punished yourselves. Would either of you like to try my pipe?"

He took another bite, swallowed and opened his mouth as if to say something else—but out came a roar of laughter. Hannah's mother joined in, Sophie and Hannah each let out a quavering "Tee-hee," then began to laugh too, until the room was practically shaking with mirth.

"Go to bed, you two. I'll help Mother with the dishes."

Sophie lay in the dark listening to Hannah's soft breathing, and promised herself, "Whenever anyone offers me a cigarette, I'll just say politely, 'No thank you,' and remember what happened when Hannah and I attempted the 'Perfect Crime'!"

12

Well, I'd better get to packing, Sophie thought. *Just two more days and Papa will be picking me up.* It would seem strange to be back on the farm again, working in the garden, herding cattle, washing clothes, hauling water from the well—even having to pump it when there was no wind to turn the windmill; endless backbreaking jobs that left her yearning for bedtime each night. Oh, well, there would be Saturday nights to look forward to, since Papa had started letting Bert drive the car and take the cream and eggs to town. Perhaps she might even be getting some dates, now that she had graduated. Would some of the farm boys think she was pretty? It was going to seem funny not to have Sarai at home. To think that she was married and expecting a baby! Sophie paused in her packing and sat down on the bed. "I want to have boyfriends, but I don't want to get married for a long time. How I hope that we have a good wheat crop this fall, so there will be money for me to go to teacher's college. . . . Then maybe, I can teach our school and stay right at home."

She stood up as her thoughts moved on. "Why wouldn't I want to get away? I love being with Papa and Mama, Bert and Robby, but I really need to spread my wings. There is a great big world out there that I know nothing about. Here on the farm, how will I ever meet young men to date, ones that I haven't known all of my life? If I did manage to meet someone new, would he want to drive all the way out here to pick me up for dates? Oh, well, I have all summer to think about it, to plan my future. I want to dance, to paint, to write. I intend to have a life stuffed with a whole lot of different experiences."

As she continued to get her winter clothes and school things packed and piled by the door, her thoughts went back to the past year: part of it is so miserable, and the last few months like a wonderful, fairy-tale dream. How happy she had been last summer, when Mama had approached Papa about renting Sophie a room for her senior year. Papa said, "What's wrong with her working for her room and board, as she has been doing? Work never hurt anyone."

Mama put her hands on her hips, which meant she intended to take a firm stand on the issue, and gave Papa a sharp look.

"She'll be back on the farm working come summer anyway, and she'll have the rest of her life to work. Perhaps if we had done this for Sarai, she might not have married so young."

Mama dropped her hands and began to roll up her apron as if she were gathering eggs in it, the way she always did when she was upset, and turned to stare out the window as she absently picked a geranium leaf off the sill. Then she turned back to Papa.

"I do so wish we had given Sarai a chance to enjoy her last year of school." Papa stood silent. At last he said, "All right. You'd better get up there and see what you can find." Then he walked out the door.

Sophie remembered how excited she had been as she glanced around the little room in Mrs. Binder's old house, listening to Mama talking to Mrs. Binder in the adjacent kitchen.

"Are you sure that the room will be warm enough in the winter?"

"Don't worry. I always bank the fire in the kitchen range at night and the door in-between will always be kept open. With her own kerosene stove to cook on and a little kerosene heater to warm the room up in a hurry in the morning, your girlie will be just fine."

It had been glorious during the fall months of her senior year. Sophie loved cooking for herself and having girlfriends over. She got to go home weekends, and Mama always sent back milk, eggs, bacon and ham, canned beef, chicken, loaves of her wonderful bread, cake, cookies, dill pickles, Million Dollar pickles; all the good food she'd grown up with. How her friends loved to come and eat with her.

But then winter came! She woke up each morning shivering no matter how many blankets she had piled on, and she could see her breath in the frosty air. There would actually be a thin film of ice on the pail of water. When she turned on the kerosene heater for warmth and the camp stove to fix oatmeal on, the odor made her so sick to her stomach that she could hardly eat, but if she opened the door to the kitchen it was only to hear it slam shut very soon. She went to school still shivering, her hands, feet and nose like ice. After school, she came home to an icy cold room. Taking a bath or keeping herself looking nice was almost impossible. If on Saturday she rinsed out clothes and hung them over the chairs to dry, they would still be damp on Sunday. At last she asked Mrs. Binder why the door wasn't left open for warmth, as promised. Mrs. Binder sniffed.

"Well, young lady, I didn't tell YOU that I would keep that door open. My daughter Minnie needs that kitchen warm so she can study. She is a smart girl. She'll be Valedictorian of her class when she graduates this year, you mark my words."

Sophie was stunned. She knew that she could herself be Valedictorian, if she only could be warm enough to study! Many nights she went down to the drug store to do homework, but it was hard to concentrate, with the high school kids all there talking and laughing.

That was an extra cold, bitter winter. Papa couldn't fetch her home from the train station on weekends, to see the family and to get Mama's good baked food and all the other thoughtful things she always had ready for Sophie. Unless Papa took the long trip to town through the snowdrifts to get a letter mailed, she didn't even get news of how they were faring. At Christmastime when it thawed a bit Papa was able to pick her up at the station, but two days after Christmas the snow began to blow again, and he had to drive her in the sleigh to catch the train and get back to school. How lovely it had been, to be home with the family, to play carrom with Bert and read stories to Robby, sitting with her feet on the warm register. Christmas goodies had never tasted so good, and she had never felt more loved. Then to return to that cold, dreary room! The first night she was back she sat on the bed as her eyes streamed with tears, both from her aching heart and from the fumes from that darn old smelly kerosene stove! For a moment she wished that she had told Papa and Mama about how miserable and cold she was, how Mrs. Binder wouldn't let her keep the door to the kitchen open. But she hadn't said a word, remembering how Mama had to talk Papa into renting her a room and how much time Mama had spent trying to find it.

Sophie had made a new friend, Barbara, and invited her over one day. Barbara looked around the room with her arms folded tightly, shivering, and said, "How can you stand being so cold? And what is that smell?"

Sophie walked over and opened the kitchen door.

"There. It should get warmer soon."

The door slammed shut before they even had a chance to take off their coats, much to Sophie's embarrassment.

"Come on, let's go over to my house," Barbara said.

What joy it was to walk into Barbara's home. It was so comfortable and bright, with the winter sun shining through the sparkling windows, touching the carpet and overstuffed sofa with golden, warm rays. They went into the kitchen, where Barbara told Sophie to sit down in the cozy breakfast nook while she fixed hot cocoa. Everything was so clean and oh, it was so warm! No sickening fumes and no crabby old woman to slam the door, shutting off any chance to be comfortable. Sophie leaned back, heaved a deep sigh and said, "I feel as if I have died and gone to heaven. How lucky you are."

The two girls sat laughing and talking over cocoa and toast, until Sophie noticed that the sun was about to set. She reluctantly stood up, thanked Barbara for the lovely treats and time, and walked out into the cold evening air.

The next afternoon she opened the door to the kitchen as soon as she got home, before taking off her coat, with very little hope that it would be left even slightly ajar. She could almost hear the loud bang already, and the angry voice on the other side lamenting about ". . . irresponsible brat." Sure enough, the door was soon closed—but softly, much to Sophie's surprise; and the voices she heard coming from the kitchen were normal in tone. She lit the burner on her little kerosene stove and held her cold hands over the flame, ignoring the heaving of her stomach from the fumes that reached her nose. One of the faint voices began to sound familiar, not like the voices that she was used to hearing from the other side of the door. Whose could it be?

Suddenly the door opened and in came Barbara! Her mother, Mrs. Brooks, was right behind her. Barbara's freckled face shined with a wide smile, but Mrs. Brooks' face was grim, quite different from her usual sweet expression.

"Sophie, gather up all of your things. We'll help you pack them. You are coming home with us. I will let your parents know, and I'm sure they won't object when they hear what has been going on here."

It didn't take long for Sophie to put everything in the boxes she had saved, with Barbara and her mother helping. As they marched out the door with their loads, Sophie heard Mrs. Binder's shrill voice.

"You'd better not carry off any of my stuff. I've been missing my best mixing bowl. Spoiled brat, going and complaining to other folks. After all I've done for you, taking you into my home and treating you like one of my own. You've not heard the last of this. Wait until I get ahold of your folks."

Sophie and Barbara both turned around and stuck out their tongues. Mrs. Brooks said, "Now girls, remember what the scriptures say."

But she was smiling as they got in the car and drove away.

It had all seemed like a wonderful dream come true, to be settled in the Brooks' home for the rest of the school year; to truly be like one of the family, to be warm, and able to take a decent bath, and eat Mrs. Brooks' wonderful food. Sophie was happy to help with the housework, and also to help Barbara with the school work that did not come easy for her.

Now she was about to leave this happy place. It seemed hardly possible that the school year was almost over and she would be going home. She would miss Barbara and her mother, but in the meantime there were a lot of things in the near future to look forward to.

A beautiful white dress made of silk moire lay on the bed, its full skirt spread out to make its waist look even tinier. The sleeves puffed happily and the turquoise buttons, marching in a row down the front, glowed in the lamplight. Sophie turned to Barbara and threw her arms around her.

"I can't believe I'm really graduating! These last few months have been just like heaven—all because of your Mama and you, rescuing me from the awful place. How can I ever pay you back? And my Mama, for making my beautiful graduation dress, of brand new material! How I wish she were here so I could hug her too!"

Sophie let go of Barbara and went whirling around the room until she stumbled over a box leaning against the wall by the door.

"Be careful," Barbara said, with a big smile and a sparkle in her green eyes. "You might be sorry if you smash that box. Maybe you should look inside."

Sophie stopped her mad whirling and picked up the box, a puzzled look on her face.

"What could it be? Where did it come from?"

"Just open it," said Barbara. "That's the best way to find out."

Sophie carried it to the bed and slowly took off the cover, almost afraid to look. She couldn't believe her eyes. Another beautiful dress! This one was made of navy blue eyelet, with a little white collar and white cuffs on short sleeves. She held it up against herself. The size looked perfect.

"Where did it come from?"

"Mother's and my graduation gift to you. Try it on and see if it fits."

Unable to say a word, she stood before the dresser mirror. Was that really herself in that mirror? Looking so grownup and . . . yes, even pretty? Sophie began to sob and sob, until Barbara told her to take the dress off before she soaked it with her tears. Two new dresses at one time! It was overwhelming. She dried her eyes, then hung the two beautiful dresses very carefully in the closet, and turned to Barbara. But Barbara had tiptoed out of the room, closing the door softly.

To be Valedictorian of the senior class had always been Sophie's dream. She had pictured herself on the stage at graduation, with the proud faces of Mama and Papa looking up at her as she delivered her speech, for which she had even written a magnificent opening sure to have everyone in the audience sitting on the edge of their seats. *Well,* she thought, *I would have made it if I hadn't been practically freezing to death in that awful room, where even trying to study was impossible.* Now here she was in this lovely warm home with these wonderful people, and she would be giving the Salutatorian's address instead—but she would still be up there on the stage in her new blue eyelet dress, making her speech, and Mama and Papa would be just as proud, oh yes. As "Poet of the Year" she would also be reading the poem she had written. And then the next night she would wear her beautiful new white dress that Mama had made to the Barn Dance that was held each year to honor the seniors. Olaf, the principal's nephew from Minnesota, who had lived here for the past year, had invited her to go with him. Oh, life was wonderful!

Olaf was a tall, lanky boy with rust-colored hair and

a Norwegian accent; shy, but with a big happy grin. He wanted to take her to the carnival that came to town every year at graduation time. Sophie hadn't made up her mind about that—but what fun it was to have a date and to be able to choose what she wanted to do. *I'm almost grown up,* she thought.

*   *   *

Sophie stumbled off the platform after giving her Salutatorian's address and reading her poem. As she took her place among the graduates, her feet ached but her heart sang. "I did it, I did it! As long as I could see Papa and Mama, Bert, and Sarai, I was all right."

Soon it was over and Sophie was standing outside the building with the family. She felt as if she were somewhere up in the sky gazing down at everyone. Had she really graduated? Olaf stood just out of the circle, his hands clasped in front of him as he stared solemnly at her. Papa was saying, ". . . don't know why she can't go home with us tonight. All that gas used and time wasted when I need to be in the fields, just to make an extra trip tomorrow."

Mama's hands were on her hips, her chin thrust forward.

"Sophie needs to be able to celebrate her graduation. My goodness, but aren't we proud of her! I can drive up after her tomorrow."

Papa's chin came out too.

"You can't drive the Model B."

Fire in her eyes, Mama responded, "I'll practice tomorrow morning, come and get her tomorrow afternoon and be home in time to help with the milking."

With that, she marched off to the car. Papa looked at Olaf, grinned and winked.

"You take good care of her, young man."

Then he followed Mama to the Model B.

Olaf shifted from one foot to the other, and looked Sophie up and down as she stood there in her beautiful white dress.

"I don't suppose you are really dressed for carnival rides. We could skip it if you want." Sophie remembered how his eyes had lit up as he talked about the carnival coming to town, how he had told her that he had never been on a Ferris wheel. She simply could not say no.

"It's okay, Olaf. Let's go. I've never been on a Ferris wheel either. I'll just be very careful of my dress. Mama made it and it would break her heart if I ruined it." . . . *and I would never forgive myself,* she thought.

The lights were so bright, the music so loud; there was so much excitement in the air, Sophie found herself holding hands with Olaf and laughing as they walked around eating cotton candy. They shot at targets, and wonder of wonders, won a teddy bear! Soon they were gazing at the Ferris wheel . . . then they were sitting on a seat, about to start their first ride ever . . . and then they were high in the air, looking down on the people moving around, so tiny from way up there. How beautiful the sky looked with the stars that twinkled almost as bright as the lights of the carnival. Sophie felt as if she were floating on a cloud. Where was her harp? Oh, she had a teddy bear instead. All at once the wheel started down and Sophie's stomach went for a spin. She stopped looking at the beautiful sky and clapped her teddy bear over her mouth. Never had she felt so sick. "Don't let me throw up!" she prayed. Olaf was gulping next to her, looking like a ghost in the artificial light. Oh, no, not him, too! Finally the awful thing stopped and they could get off. Olaf headed for a bench with Sophie right behind him, still holding the teddy bear over her mouth. She didn't know if she dared put it down.

"Are you all right?" came a weak voice.

"I guess so," Sophie answered.

They turned to look at each other. *I wonder if I look as bad as he does?* she thought, and let out a weak giggle. The next moment both of them were laughing and laughing as they clutched their roiling stomachs. How romantic! To get sick on graduation night, on her first date with Olaf.

Olaf had his uncle's car, and as they drove to the Barn Dance they talked about their plans for the future. He would be going to Minneapolis to go to college. Sophie didn't tell him that whether she started college in the fall or not depended on how the wheat crop turned out. She did say that she would probably study to be an elementary-school teacher, but she didn't mention how all her life she had dreamed of being a famous dancer, artist, and writer—all three.

The dance was held in the haymow of a big red barn. Music blared from fiddle, guitar and a tiny old piano that had been laboriously hauled up the rough steps to the loft, where the band sat on bales of hay and stomped their feet to the tunes as they played. The crowd was not the usual barn-dance mix of young and old in overalls and gingham dresses; instead, teenagers in their graduation finery swirled around the floor. Sophie had that dream-like feeling again. How strange it was to be dancing in her beautiful dress, after surviving a scary Ferris wheel ride, saved by a stuffed bear from leaving her dinner behind a bush or on the dress itself . . . and how wonderful it was to be waving and smiling at all of these friends who had shared the last four years with her, and to be in the arms of a tall young man who made her feel very special. Even the thought of the ride home, in a car very different from Papa's Model B, made shivers of pure delight run up and down her back.

When they were home, when Olaf walked her to the door and looked down at her, her heart nearly stopped. Was he going to kiss her? Should she let him? He just stood there for a minute, shifting from one foot to the other as his face got redder and redder, until at last he said, "If you want to give me your address, I'll write to you from college . . . if you'll answer."

Sophie ran into the house for a piece of paper and a pencil. A wild-looking head of red hair rose up from the sofa, and Barbara's sleepy voice whispered, "How was it? Did you neck?"

"Barbara!"

Sophie ran back outside.

"Here is some paper. It was all I could find."

She giggled as she scribbled her address on a scrap torn from a brown paper bag and handed it to Olaf, who stuffed it in his pocket. He hesitated. Then he took her hand and squeezed it, shook it, turned abruptly and strode down the sidewalk, tripping slightly over a rough spot, to the car where he folded his lanky length inside and drove off.

"Thank you, oh thank you for a wonderful time," called Sophie to the rear lights disappearing rapidly down the street.

13

The blazing sun beat down relentlessly on the tin roof of the old truck. Sophie was trying to steer it across the stubble field with one hand on the wheel, while with the other hand she wiped the sweat from her face with one of Papa's red bandanas. The going was rough. The big dishpan on the passenger's seat, loaded with chicken sandwiches, rolled from side to side and threatened to spill the sandwiches onto the dirty floor. She could hear the lemonade sloshing in the five-gallon cream can that sat in the truck bed. If only she could reach the comparative shade of the straw stack before it tipped over. Oh, the noise and dust! The big old threshing machine lumbered and roared as the crew tossed the shocks of wheat into its yawning mouth, while a stream of wheat kernels poured from it into Papa's wagon standing ready with its team of horses, and the straw spewed out on the ground to form another straw stack. The moment Papa's wagon started for the granary with its load to be stored for next year's planting, one of the Johnson boys would take his place, backing his truck up to catch the grain that continued to pour out. When he had a full load, he would drive to town and sell it. Both Bert and Eric Johnson were on the threshing crew this year.

Just as Sophie jerked to a halt by the straw-stack, Robby came running up. One knee of his overalls was torn, his face was dirty and streaked where the sweat had rolled down, and he looked as if he had butted his head into the straw stack.

"Soph, Soph," he yelled. "The threshing machine is stopping and all the men are ready to eat. May I have a sandwich and lemonade too? I've been helping, when they let me anyway." Sophie smiled as she picked straw out of his hair.

"Of course you can. Now, run and tell the men it's time for lunch. That will be helping." Robby set out at a run, yelling as he tried to push half a sandwich into his mouth at the same time.

"Come and eat! My sister says it's time."

The noisy machine had stopped and the men talked and laughed as they headed to the truck. What a relief to be able to hear their voices, to hear even the trill of a meadowlark as it flew off a fence post. Sophie let the tailgate of the truck down and put the dishpan of sandwiches next to the lemonade and drinking cups. She sat down on the running-board and looked out over the golden stubble field. Would the crop be good enough, and the price of wheat high enough, so that after Mama sent to Sears Roebuck for all of the dried food and winter clothing, there would still be money for her to go to college? "Oh, please, heavenly Father," she prayed, "I need to go." Her hopes soared as she heard the men talking as they ate.

"What a wheat crop," came Eric's voice. "Bert, if the price hangs in there you'll be so rich you won't want to even speak to us poor folks. Thirty bushels to the acre, at least."

After a pause, another voice remarked, "It must be at least 100 degrees today, and the forecast calls for even hotter tomorrow."

There were groans at this, then nothing to be heard but chicken sandwiches being munched.

The crew began to straggle back to work, but Bert stretched and yawned. He put his empty cup on the tailgate, smiled at Sophie and said, "You won't tell Pa if I take just a wee bit of a nap behind a shock, will you?" Sophie grinned and came back at him:

"What if I told about that cream can? The one that you promised to pick up from the depot, if Papa would let you use the car to go to the dance? It never did arrive home. He'd probably like to find out whatever happened to it. Is it behind a shock?"

"Okay," Bert retorted. "Maybe I should tell him about what I heard you whispering to Sarai! Which Johnson boy's the best kisser, huh?"

Sophie's and Bert's faces both turned even redder than they were already in the hot sun. Bert put his arm around Sophie as she gave her brother a peck on the cheek and said, "I won't tell if you won't tell. Promise?"

"Yeah, promise," Bert said, then ran to catch up with the rest of the crew as the loud rumble filled the air once more.

* * *

Robby tweaked Mama's apron-string as she leaned over the dish pan of sudsy water.

"Mama, I'm supposed to bring some hot water out to the barn for some of those men who are threshing here. They said they needed to soak their sore feet because they have to walk so much. Oh, Mama, could I sleep out in the hayloft with them just one night?"

"We'll see, Robby. What if you fell down the hole into Sunday Biscuit's manger again, the way you did when you were little?"

Robby grinned.

"Well, it's too hot to wear red mittens now, and besides, we don't have Sunday Biscuit anymore."

Mama put a large kettle of hot water in Robby's wagon and he went gleefully down the rocky path to the barn, slopping a good share of the water out on the way. A while later he came back into the kitchen, his eyes as big as saucers.

"Mama, I didn't fall down the hay hole and the men didn't soak their feet in that water. That man who asked me for the water poured something into it from a big bottle, and then they all drank some of it, and they told me to go back to the house. Now they are all laughing and singing funny songs."

Mama stood with her hands on her hips.

"Don't you go out there again. Papa will tend to this."

Sophie had just come up from the cellar with a big pan of potatoes and carrots for tomorrow's dinner. Never had she heard such loud singing and laughing, she thought as she watched Papa heading down to the barn. Soon he came back to the house, his mouth grim but with a little twinkle in his eyes.

"Well, Mama, it's a good thing those men will be finishing up here tomorrow and moving on. That is, if they're able to get out into the field. Have Bert and Eric gone to bed already? They'll probably be the only ones who put in a good day's work tomorrow. I think they'd better find a different crew to work with." He handed Mama the kettle. "Tomorrow those fellows will be doing their 'foot soaking' right here by the lean-to, where they do their washing up."

When the threshers had first arrived the dining room table was extended with leaves as far as it would go, but there were still not enough chairs to set fourteen men; so Papa brought in long two-by-fours the same length as the table and laid their ends on chairs to form benches on both sides of the table. Smart Papa.

Sophie noticed Peter the first day of threshing, when he smiled at her. What white, even teeth he had. Next day at breakfast he said, "Good morning." After that, he smiled and spoke to her at every meal, and last night at dinner he said, "Those were good sandwiches you made."

What an opportunity. But Papa had said sternly, before threshing started: "Sophie, I don't want you getting friendly with any of these men. We don't know anything about them."

Surely he didn't mean just sitting down for a minute and smiling back. That wasn't "getting friendly," was it? She put down a dish of butter, reached under the end of the heavy board to adjust it, and sat down on it with her best smile—which abruptly changed to a look of perfect horror. Her fingers were still between the end of the board and the chair seat. With an unearthly scream she leaped up and ran sobbing to the kitchen.

The men were still filing into the room.

"What happened?"

"Did somebody get hurt?"

"Pete, did you try to kiss that sweet young lady?"

Tears were pouring down Sophie's face as she held her hand in cold water and bit her lip to keep from moaning. Papa and Robby helped Mama serve dinner and wash up, and Sophie insisted on doing all she could, but how those poor fingers hurt. After she set the table for breakfast, peeled potatoes and carrots and left them in water, brought up jars of peaches, and checked the dough rising for tomorrow's bread, she climbed wearily up the stairs, flexing her sore fingers as she went. She lay in bed thinking of how embarrassing it had been. "I hope Mama will wait on table tomorrow, and let me dish up and wash dishes." Over and over in her mind the scene played. How could she ever live it down? "I can never face Peter again. But oh! He is so handsome."

The next day the threshers finished up and left. How nice and quiet it became. The dining room table was back to its normal size, the boards taken away. The family sat down to talk about the past week as they ate a happy meal together. Sophie's fingers still hurt, and she announced to the rest of the family, "Well, I'll never try to get friendly with a strange man again—even if he is handsome and has beautiful teeth."

On the following day Papa took the last load of wheat to town. It was getting late and supper was ready by the time he got home. It seemed to take forever for him to let the weary team out to graze, wash up, come in the house and join everyone else at the dining room table, with an expression on his face as if he had a big secret. What was on Papa's mind? They all looked at him, waiting for him to share. Had the price of wheat gone way down? Was there no room for the wheat in the town elevator?

"Papa," said Robby, "you had better share. You always make me tell my secrets, so that if I've been bad I can be punished. Is your secret good or bad?"

"Well," said Papa, "it all depends on how you look at it."

He got up from his chair, walked over to Sophie, and laid his hand on her head.

"Sophie girl, we're really going to miss you when you head off for college. You'd better start your packing."

* * *

Sophie was ready to go. She wondered what she might have forgotten in her excitement; probably something that she couldn't possibly do without. Mama was outdoors instructing Papa on how to arrange Sophie's luggage in the Model B in which Mama would take her to the train station, having become an expert at driving Papa's pride and joy—much as he hated to admit it. Sophie thought of how he had come into her room that morning while she was packing, put his arm around her and said, "Be a good girl," and walked out quickly. As he left, she saw him pull his big, old, red handkerchief out of his pocket and wipe his eyes. Dear Papa. He should have wiped her brimming eyes, too. Sitting down on the bed, she looked around the room that had been at first both hers and Sarai's, then just hers to find refuge in, to dream in, to cry in—and of course, to try on her beautiful, too tight Roman boots! Would she ever forget that heart-wrenching experience? The memories seemed more real than the present moment. She felt as if she were in a dream and would wake up any minute to find herself out by the haystack, serving chicken sandwiches to tired, dirty men.

Sophie got up and shook herself to stop the trembling. Firmly she said out loud, to herself and anyone else who might be listening, "But it's true. It's really true. I am going away to college. I'll miss Papa and Mama, Sarai and Little Bert, Big Bert and Robby, but I'm really going!"

She walked over to the east window, opened it wide, leaned out as far as she dared and shouted at the top of her voice, "World. Here I come!"

14

She sat in the spacious old rocking chair, her wrinkled hands lying relaxed in her lap. The birds and squirrels chattered outside the window, and Sophie watched them coming down from the woods above the house, launching themselves from the stone wall on their way to the dishes of sunflower seeds and bread on the picnic table. How many years had she used this chair, with the same white Afghan and plump pillow, as a retreat where she could sit to rest a bit or listen to records played on the stereo that had stood so long under the dining room window. So many times she had put on "String of Pearls," played by Glenn Miller of course, and pulled a reluctant Bill into the dining room to dance. *What fun we used to have,* she thought, *dancing at the Elks Club on Friday night, then stopping at the ice cream parlor for cones—was there ever anything better than pralines-and-cream? Perhaps I should put a record on right now and get up and dance, just to see if I still can. . . .* but then other memories came rushing in and she sank back into the comfort of the friendly old chair.

She closed her eyes and thought of her children. When she was young, dreaming of being a famous author, an artist, a dancer, or all three, she hadn't realized how children can be more precious than an all-consuming career. Some of her stories, poems and songs had been published; her paintings still hung on her walls—but what about the dancing dream? "Well . . . I guess I was lucky to be able to dance the Rumba to 'Blue Spanish Eyes' the night Bill and I met."

Sophie raised her hands to the sunlight streaming in the window. When did they get so ancient-looking? She remembered how once as a child, she had drawn around her hand to show Papa how well she could draw. He had picked up both her hands in one of his and said, "Sophie girl, with these sturdy little hands you will always have to work for a living."

"Yes, Papa, and I did," she now said softly. "I lived and worked through heartache and disappointment, joy and ecstasy. Now I live on memories."

Her thoughts went on. "I'll never forget that day so long ago, when I had just finished packing for my first year of college. How young I was. How willing to meet any challenge, as I opened my bedroom window, leaned out and shouted to the World to get ready!

"Are my memories the same as my children's? Probably not. I always felt that the most important thing was to love, and perhaps sometimes I loved unwisely. My children, my grandchildren, my great-grandchildren, I loved them so much . . . was it enough? Was it too much? I tried so hard to be a good mother. How do we really know if we have succeeded? It seemed important to be myself, to give to my children all that I had to give that was right and good, and to help them recognize and discard what was foolish and wrong in the world. . . ."

Sophie closed her eyes. She let a poem that she had written many years ago fill her heart and mind.

To My Children:
To you I give a legacy, not boxed or wrapped, it's not
    that kind of gift.

      I give you courage.
Not a banner waving, bright red kind, but a 'me' kind
Scared to death but grit your teeth and forge ahead
    variety.
My needs have lessened but your needs are great.
I do not give an equal share to each. How do I know
    whose needs are greater?
I know you'll share, you always have, the four of you.
        This I do ask
That each of you will keep yours bright and whole and
    pass it on
        My gift to you, unboxed, unwrapped.
        With love and prayers
Your Mom

Sophie felt tears filling her eyes and wiped them away, realizing how tired she was. She dozed off for just a few minutes, then woke with a start, raised herself slowly from the old rocking chair, and said to no one at all, "Then . . . are the children free."